A FIRESIDE BOOK

PUBLISHED BY SIMON & SCHUSTER, INC.
NEW YORK

# CITY KIDS

RAISE KIDS IN URBAN AREAS—FROM
CINCINNATI TO SEATTLE—AND HAVE FUN
DOING IT

SUSAN HAVEN

VALERIE MONROE

A FIRESIDE BOOK

Published by Simon & Schuster, Inc.
Simon & Schuster Building
Rockefeller Center
1230 Avenue of the Americas
New York, NY 10020

FIRESIDE and colophon are registered trademarks of
Simon & Schuster, Inc.

Manufactured in the United States of America

10   9   8   7   6   5   4   3   2   1

Library of Congress Cataloging in Publication Data

Haven, Susan.
  City kids.

  "A Fireside book."
  Bibliography: p.
  1. Child rearing—United States—Handbooks, manuals, etc.   2. Parenting—United States—Handbooks,
manuals, etc.   3. City children—United States—Handbooks, manuals, etc.   I. Monroe, Valerie.   II. Title.
HQ769.H398   1987      649'.1        87-17811

ISBN 0-671-64673-7

# ACKNOWLEDGMENTS

Our thanks to Bob Bender, Judy Berezin, Annie Clarke, Carolyn Enriquez, Mark Haven, Dr. Elaine Heffner, Jonina Herter, Bernice Kaufman, Dr. Ralph Lopez, Elisa Petrini, Nancy Pike, Roberta Pryor, Barbara Reisman, Jack Sasaki, and the counseling service staff of the Hudson Guild Mental Health Clinic, Dr. June Schwartz, Keith Sheridan, David Shookhoff, Susan Springer, Barbara Stern, Lester and Connie Trimble, Dr. Jessie Turberg, Randy Williams, Shirley Wright, Laura Yorke; and to all of the city parents and city kids who generously shared their time and their insights with us.

Raising children in cities offers them diverse opportunities. These kids are enjoying themselves, immersed in nature and art, at Logan Square in Philadelphia. (PHOTO BY RICHARD STEEDMAN)

*For Paul and for Reid*

# CONTENTS

# INTRODUCTION

We are the mothers of a fifteen-year-old son and a three-year-old son. We are city parents; our children are city kids. We have made the decision to live in the center of a large city because we love it here. We love the variety, the energy, the opportunity, the stimulation, the fun. Although we sometimes wonder how our children's lives might be different if we lived in the suburbs or in the country, we know that we want to raise our children here. For all its pros and cons, we feel sure that a city childhood can be an exciting and fulfilling odyssey.

But looking back on Paul's childhood and looking ahead to Reid's, we have both realized a tremendous need: a need for guideposts for parents of the city child. Raising a child in the city is different from raising a child in the suburbs or in the country—and different from what it was like only fifteen or twenty years ago. Urban parents are pioneers. If we're not first-generation city parents, the likelihood is that the city we were raised in has changed significantly since our childhoods. In addition, family life is different today than it was when we were children.

As pioneers, we're faced with the excitement and exhilaration of an uncharted life. But we are also faced with the feelings of insecurity that came from a lack of role models, as well as the need to solve new problems daily. If we've moved to cities because life there is interesting and unpredictable, we've found that our lives are—well, unpredictable.

So we wind up feeling ambivalent about having chosen urban childhoods for our kids. If, on top of that, we have the common inclination to glorify our own childhoods, we find ourselves wanting our children to have the sense of freedom we remember having; the sense that even if the world wasn't safe, our block or our house truly was. But living in cities today, we can't possibly meet these ideals. Our expectations are unrealistic for the way we live. And our ambivalence is further exacerbated by a national fondness for life in Lake Wobegon. We feel there is a bias against raising kids in cities: It's not the American way.

Yet one in every four people in New York, Chicago, Los Angeles, Cincinnati, Philadelphia, Detroit and most other big cities is a child.

We wanted this book to deal with the experience of what it's like to be a middle-class city parent raising a child today. We wanted the answers to practical questions about how to raise our city kids best—questions such as: How does a new city parent negotiate the city with a baby? How does she survive playground life, or maybe even come to enjoy it? How does she meet other parents, find day care or hire a babysitter or housekeeper? How does she choose a school? How does she resolve the problems of raising children mostly indoors, in small spaces? How do we provide our kids with an active outdoor life? How does a child handle transportation in the city during different stages of his life? How does a parent—or should one—protect a child from exposure to the unpleasant side of city life, from pornography to the mentally ill? How can we ensure that our children partake of our city's cultural riches, from the music it offers and the theatre and the fine arts to the variety of ethnic cultures?

We went to city parents and to experts familiar with the city childhood experience for our answers. And of course, we went to city kids. This book is a collection of their ideas—a collection, finally, of folk wisdom, supported by expert advice.

But not just advice. We also found a powerful affirmation of urban childhood. Most experienced parents, and nearly every city child we spoke to, were happy about the way city kids turn out. They pointed out that, though it was hard in some ways to grow up in the city, a certain kind of city child is a common breed: The child who plays baseball *and* the cello, who is both sophisticated *and* innocent, who has a sense that there are many kinds of people in the world, who explores vibrant neighborhoods—a child who has been nourished by the experience of living in the midst of political, social, and cultural activity.

If it's great to be a city kid but not always easy, neither is it easy to be a city parent. If city kids are sophisticated, that means that we parents have to help them assimilate the increased information they inexorably absorb. If they are street smart, that means that while they're getting that way, we worry about their safety and physical and mental well-being.

Essentially, city kids are a neglected part of the urban community. We believe that though many of the people who live in our cities love children, the people who run them don't. After all, children are a constituency with no voice. Why is it difficult to negotiate many public and private buildings with a stroller? Why isn't there reduced fare on public transportation for our adolescent children? If a successful park is one that integrates all members of a community, why are mothers with babies often isolated in city playgrounds? When one out of every four citizens in our major cities is a child, why are our city's public schools severely neglected?

If our children's concerns and our concerns about them are to be addressed, we have to make them heard. We have to help shape our children's environment. The bigger the city we live in, the less manageable that seems. But we have been told again and again that the way to tackle almost any city problem is to create a community and to use the collective power that comes from it. City parents and city kids are already a large community. We hope this book, which reflects the experiences of hundreds of city families, conveys that feeling and so provides realistic help and comfort to those of us living on the urban front.

# CHAPTER 1

# STROLLERING THE CITY

*T*he first time I took my two-month-old son out onto the streets of the Northside, I felt just as I did as a little girl, playing house, pushing my doll in her carriage. I felt ridiculously happy and, being a former career woman, also a bit ridiculous. It was tough to take myself seriously as a mother right away.

—Judith M., Chicago

*W*heeling Peter in his stroller marked a change in our relationship. Before then, with the Snugli or the backpack, we were one unit. Now, for the first time in public, we were separate people. That was both frightening, because he was much more vulnerable to everything on the street, and satisfying, because he was more noticeable, too; and countless people stopped to tell me countless appealing things about him.

—Caitlin R., Brooklyn, New York

*O*nce you get the hang of getting around with a stroller with your toddler, you begin to realize why you wanted to raise kids in the city in the first place. Every time you go out, something's different. And every time you're alone in the house and going crazy, you can take a walk down the street and see a lot of people. If you're home with kids all day, that can be a life saver.

—Judy W., Rochester, New York

Getting out on the streets of your city with your child marks the beginning of raising a city kid. It's "going public" as a city mother for the first time. It's your first exposure as a city parent to the essence of what makes the urban experience special. And it's your first opportunity as a parent to be out there in the rich, energetic, varied, unpredictable, noisy, hectic street. It's your opportunity to begin to teach your child how to become street smart, to introduce him to his home town, and, corny as it sounds, to begin teaching him about life. As Jane Jacobs has written in *The Death and Life of Great American Cities* (New York: Random House, 1961), "Streets and their sidewalks, the main public places of a city, are its most vital organs. If a city's streets look interesting, the city looks interesting; if they look dull, the city looks dull."

16

Cities, Jacobs points out, "are not like towns, only larger. They are not like suburbs, only denser. They differ in basic ways and one of these is that cities are, by definition, full of strangers."

And when you begin strollering, you will feel as if you are being confronted by all of them. One of the first things you become aware of is that you are now one of the most approachable of city creatures. There is something about a woman pushing a child in a stroller that makes her unconditionally available for conversation. You are advised by philosophers: "Babies are God's gift to the world"; by cautionaries: "Little people, little problems, big people, big problems"; and by critics: "Put on his hat, he's cold. Take off his blanket, he's hot." Where once you were an anonymous adult or part of an anonymous couple, you're now one of the city's main attractions.

It's a mixed urban blessing. Karen, mother of an eighteen-month-old, told us, "Since I've always loved to talk and had fewer opportunities for adult conversations since Willy's birth, I was pleased with nearly all unsolicited approaches." But not all mothers are. "I felt as if I were being assaulted," reported another mother. "I couldn't take Ellen anywhere without someone giving me advice about how I should raise her, or criticism about how I had dressed her. Some days I dreaded going out. All I ever felt like saying was, 'Aaah, shuddup.'" There comes a point, many mothers agree, when the only thing you can do to keep your sanity is to nod and smile and keep walking, even if you feel you're being rude.

Being out on the streets with your child is really the beginning of your social life as a mother. Many mothers feel as if they've just joined a club, a subculture they never much noticed before. The most common get-acquainted line is not "What do you do?"—(which is obvious)—but "How old is your baby?"

"I felt so vulnerable at first," says a mother of two toddlers. "I'd approach any mother who looked less sure of herself than I did." For a lot of women, that's how first mother friends are made.

---

## WHAT KIND OF STROLLER IS BEST FOR CITY USE?

In the city, especially, it makes a big difference what kind of stroller you buy. The sidewalks are crowded, and you are constantly negotiating bumps, detours, and curbs. If you use public transportation or taxis, the weight and foldability of the stroller is important, too. You'll want to invest in a good stroller from the start; it'll save you money in the long run. Your first impulse anyway, especially if this is your first baby, is to buy the best, but that doesn't necessarily translate into the most expensive.

We found—and all of the city parents we spoke to agreed—that the Maclaren strollers are the lightest, most flexible, and easiest to manage for city use. Their one drawback is that if you carry a lot of stuff in the convenient pouch you can clip onto the back, the stroller will tip over when you take your child out. A city father who likes his shoes complained that the stroller scuffed them when he kicked up the bottom to fold it.

## POLLUTION

Many of us may have thought about lousy city air before we had our city kids, but as with almost everything else, after our kids are born we began thinking about it in a different way. You take your brand-new, freshly minted infant outside for a walk, and you just don't want her breathing in diesel fuel. It's only natural. If you've ever knelt down to talk to your toddler as he's sitting in his stroller on the sidewalk, you've seen how suffocatingly close his face can get to the exhaust pipes of passing buses and cars.

Serious air pollution can make your child cranky and physically sick. Penelope Leach points out in her terrific book, *Your Growing Child* (New York: Alfred Knopf, 1986) that in addition to breathing in noxious fumes, city dwellers also inhale soot, ash, and dust. The figures she gives in tonnage are amazing: 18,000 tons of dirt in the air over Manhattan each year; 43,000 tons of it over St. Louis; and more over Los Angeles.

Apart from lobbying to improve our environment, there are things you can do to protect your child. Leach suggests these guidelines:

- Try not to take a baby shopping in a packed main street in still, muggy weather.
- Avoid long periods in a car stuck in a traffic jam; or keep the car windows closed and the air conditioning on.
- Heed warnings of local smog conditions.
- If you live in a highly polluted part of the city, you

might think of enrolling your child in a school in another area.

- At home, don't smoke; try to organize the rooms so
  that your child spends most of her time in the part of
  the house away from the street; and on smoggy days,
  keep your windows closed and the air conditioning
  on, if possible.
- Try to get your child out of the city when the air is bad
  (especially in summers) as much as possible.

## GETTING TO KNOW YOUR CITY

Especially if, prior to having your baby, you've worked a
nine-to-five job, being out on the streets during the day adds a
new dimension to city life. You have a chance to rediscover
your city. We recommend buying local tourist books, taking
local tours and in general, trying to see things from a new
perspective. One mother who's raising her daughter in Manhattan says, "When I was working full time I had neither the
time nor the inclination to take advantage of what this city
offers. But with my daughter, I carry my guidebook and I take
the ferry, go to the museums, visit the parks and the seaport.
Half the time my daughter's asleep. But she's my excuse and
my companion. I think she's getting something out of it, but
right now I'm actually doing this for myself."

If you do venture out of your neighborhood, then you have
to be prepared to be a little bit of an exhibitionist. Your child
might cry, might need to be changed or fed, might get cranky.
If you find it too stressful to handle your child's needs and
moods in public, stay near home base. It's smart to know your
own limits, and there will still be plenty to see.

For your infant and, later, your toddler, there is probably no more stimulating adventure than exploring your own neighborhood. One mother remembers, "I don't think I really knew I had a neighborhood until I had Ryan; it wasn't until then that I began to notice the people who surrounded us, who they were, what their jobs were. As the lives of the people on our block began to unfold and the city became more interesting to me, I began to communicate that interest to my son. Because of that, just about everything around us became a kind of educational tool."

A city neighborhood is a microcosm of the world. Unlike the suburbs where many of us grew up, there are men around all day; there are businesspeople of every occupation and people from different neighborhoods or different countries.

Your toddler gives you license like no other to use your neighborhood. Says one city mother: "Eric's always been a very friendly kid; he gave me the motivation and the courage to approach people on my block I never would have spoken to. For example, there's a parking lot next to our building. The attendant always made a small fuss over Eric when we walked by, and Eric loved him. One day, I asked him a favor: Could Eric sit in his little house and 'help' him? The attendant was thrilled. Eric sat on his chair, took people's tickets, and watched the attendant get people's cars and park them. He was learning about the concept of time and about money—and also about friendliness. It amazed me: I've never seen people more delighted to leave their cars or to pick them up than when they were negotiating with a two-year-old."

For every city store with a friendly owner, there's an opportunity for you and your child. A city mother remembers that, one day, when her daughter was at the age that she was fascinated by keys, she had to stop at a locksmith to have some duplicates made. As she watched the locksmith make one key and, dissatisfied with it, toss it aside, it occurred to her that he might have more junk keys he didn't need. So she asked him if he had a few extra keys she could give her daughter; he had plenty, some in shapes neither she nor her daughter had ever seen. She bought her a key ring with a huge Plexiglas initial on it, threaded it through about a dozen keys—and presto! For the cost of a key ring her little girl had a new toy she was happy with. Whenever they pass the locksmith, they go in for one more key to add to her ring.

### SAFE STREET GAMES FOR TODDLERS
When your child is at the "What's that?" stage, a walk down almost any city block is a game. Either your child asks or you point. Every mother remembers when her toddler begins to call out wildly from his stroller, "Fish!" "Bus!" "Flowers!"— and "Daddy!" at every passing man. As your toddler gets older, the instinct for inventing street games will develop in both of you. You may have your own games. Here are some reported to us:

*THE RED LIGHT GAME,* fondly remembered by one mother, who told us, "It was really sneaky of me, but my two-year-old loved it. We'd approach a corner with a red light. And I'd say, "I'm going to make that light turn green by the time I count to ten. And then we'd count to ten together—and, of course, the light would change. I'd be looking at the lights changing on the next block."
*WHERE IS IT?* was mentioned by several mothers as a variation of "What's that?" You look around for an object, then turn around and innocently ask your child, "I think I just saw the biggest red car carrier in the world. Where is it?"
*STORE WINDOW GAMES* come in infinitely entertaining variations. The simplest: Stop at a drugstore window, point to

objects, and ask your child to name the color, to find the littlest thing in the window or the biggest thing. As your child's ability to remember increases, windows become a wonderful resource for memory games. Stop at any display, let your child stare for as long as he or she wants, and then walk away together. Now ask such questions as, "I saw a big sign in the window that said *S-A-L-E*. What color was it?" You can also let your child test you. Your kid will probably do better than you, but it still can be fun.

*WHAT DID JOHNNY HAVE IN HIS POCKET?*— the city version. As you walk, you choose one object on each block and add to it from block to block. On one block you say, "I see a big man with a funny hat..." and then on the next block you add, "I see a bunch of yellow bananas *and* a big man with a funny hat..." As the city mother who suggested it says, this game can show you how your child is absorbing his city experiences. "One day," she told us, "My son was playing this game and the second thing he mentioned was 'There's a man with one leg...' That didn't faze him at all. But on the next block he said, 'And there's a lady that doesn't have any money or a place to live...' It was a street person he saw, and we had the opportunity to talk about street people and how we feel about them."

---

## TAXIS

A mother of two stroller-age children told us: "You want to hail a cab when you've got two kids and a stroller? Fine. The first thing you do is find a mailbox. Hide your stroller behind it. When a cab stops, first open the door. This prevents a reluctant cabbie from driving away when you run back to the mailbox to fetch your stroller. I haven't lost a ride yet."

Still, many cab drivers will happily let you stash a stroller in the trunk, and a lot of women reported experiences, like ours, of cab drivers who loaded and unloaded taxis, held children, or even got out to open doors and to usher mothers and children safely indoors. Admittedly, a decent tip helps, and so does a request for help. But sometimes cab drivers are just so goodhearted and understanding that it's hard to believe. One woman told us she was taking her eight-month-old with her to dinner at a friend's house, "And for some obscure reason I took just about every piece of equipment John owned. I took the big bag, of course, with his bottles and diapers, a change of clothes in case he had an accident, the little carry cradle he sometimes slept in, and his sassy seat. Somehow I managed to get into the cab all right, but when we got to my friend's house, I was wedged in the back seat. I couldn't move. 'Just a minute, just a minute,' I kept saying, shifting my weight and moving all of these stupid things around. I could not get out. Finally, the driver caught on. He opened my door and carefully removed everything from the back seat and put it on the roof of the cab. He took my son and held him while I got out and hung everything off me, then handed John back to me when I looked steady enough to walk. I could barely thank him, I was so astonished."

## THE FACTS OF STREET LIFE

Any mother who's wheeled her child around in a city knows that there comes a time when the toddler, fanatical about practicing walking, decides singlemindedly that he or she wants to get out of the stroller. No thousands of rice cakes or bottles of juice can keep him strapped and satisfied in his seat. What do you do? You can let your child scream, of course, and then you might as well wear a sandwich sign: BAD MOTHER/CHILD ABUSER. We've actually seen mothers with enough aplomb not to be bothered by a child's hysteria in public. But it usually makes us feel terrible. There is one thing it helps to think of if your child is having a tantrum in a public place—you are not at a black-tie dinner at the White House. You and your child have as much right to be wherever you are as the gentleman who is looking at you as if the two of you were mud wrestling naked on the sidewalk. Although your child's behavior may not seem appropriate and certainly is not convenient, it is natural behavior for a toddler. It is your job—and it's a legitimate job—to help your child through it.

If you decide to let your child out of the stroller, depending on his or her age, it will either take you six times as long as it usually does to get anywhere or else you will go somewhere very fast—but not where you intended. You may be the kind of person who doesn't mind at all changing your plans, many times, at the last minute. But even if you are, walking down a street with a toddler can be trying. It's no use rushing him; he's going to be distracted by everything. You can either think of this situation as a dilemma or you can use it as an opportunity to enjoy yourselves. But first, you've got to change the way you are accustomed to thinking about time. A toddler walking the streets is beginning to enjoy his town intensely. He needs time to do that. He is also beginning to learn about city survival.

Now is the time when you will begin to communicate everything you know about how to behave on the street. Even if you are not the type of person who relishes picking up old cigarette butts and popping them in your mouth, your child most assuredly will be. You've never done that, at least not in front of him; where did he learn it? Try to remember that the inclination to taste anything the entire population of the city has stepped on is the result of one of your child's most wonderful attributes—his curiosity. If it weren't for his curiosity,

If it weren't for children's curiosity, they'd never learn anything. (PHOTO BY SUZANNE OPTON)

he'd never learn anything. Your child is going to want to taste, greet, or pet just about everything he encounters—and that seems, and sometimes is, dangerous. One mother couldn't forget—though she tried—the first time her son walked along a street on New York City's Upper West Side. "He was only about ten months old, and someone of that size looks as if he has no business walking anyway," she told us. "It was the kind of crisp fall day that in New York is marred only by various kinds of debris—crusty old newspapers and such—blowing around your ankles and, if you're very short, your lips. I guess it saved Jan the trouble of having to bend down to taste everything, but for me it was a nightmare. I followed him down Columbus Avenue on my haunches, alternately shouting, 'Dirty! Dirty!' and snatching disgusting things out of his hands and brushing them off his mouth. God only knows what he ingested, but it didn't kill him. He didn't even get sick. And a few days later he said his first word—'doorty.' I was charmed."

The fact is, after a while—and we won't tell you how long in case you haven't been through this yet—your kid will stop picking up objects and begin to relate to more acceptable things on the street—other people, for example, and children, and animals. You'll notice that your child is much less discriminating than you are about whom he chooses to approach. Again, if you can remember that curiosity is basically a positive element of your child's behavior and that it is your job not only to protect him but also to help him understand the various responses to his approaches, both of your experiences will be enhanced. By your own example, you will be teaching your child how to behave on the street. If he's not cautious enough about approaching dogs, for instance, make a point of asking the animals' owner, "Is he friendly?" so that your child can plainly hear. Your child will eventually imitate your questions.

Many mothers have reported, to their confusion and dismay, that street people are often elements of interest and delight to their children. As your child begins to ask questions about them, it's important that you convey the truth of the matter at the appropriate level. Dr. Elaine Heffner, senior lecturer of education in psychiatry, Cornell University Medical College, and author of *Mothering* (New York: Doubleday/Anchor, 1978), told us that, when your child begins to ask questions, it's best to answer in a matter-of-fact, nonthreatening way. "There are certain kinds of information that must be imparted with neutrality," she says. "You have to be the judge of how much your child needs to know. If a child asks, for example, 'Why is that man sleeping on the sidewalk?' you might tell him that some people are very poor and have nowhere else to sleep. If a young child asks why a street person is muttering to herself or acting strangely, you might say that the person isn't feeling well. A panhandler might approach you or a drunk might get in your way, but out of these kinds of experiences you can begin to tell your child about some of the elements that make up life in the city. What are you doing? You are educating your child in the context of the real world."

## STREET RULES

Once your child is climbing out of his stroller, it's time to teach him about crossing the street, negotiating traffic, and watching out for bikes as well as cars. One mother, after spending several weeks teaching her toddler how to get down her front steps ("Go up to the edge and sit down") saw that her daughter used the same approach on curbs. You want to convey to your child that he should stop automatically at all street corners; but you do not want to scare him to death. Maybe this seems obvious to you; but we've seen mothers screaming "Stop! Stop at the corner, Anthony!" with mortal terror in their voices. No doubt about it, this method works. But there are less stressful ways to get your child to stop. When you're no longer constantly holding your child's hand on the sidewalk, you can begin to play corner games: "Take twelve steps to the corner and *stop!* Ride your motorcycle to the corner and *stop!* Have a walking race to the corner and *stop!*"

Above all else, you want your own and your child's first experiences walking around the city to be pleasant ones. If you can remember that your pace is going to be different from almost everyone else's, that this is a time for you and your child to be exploring and to begin to get to know the city, you will be able to turn almost any potentially negative experience into a more positive one. As one mother remembers: "I was late to meet a friend one morning, and in a New York kind of rush. I was wheeling Dennis as quickly as I could when we reached a corner I couldn't get around. A dumpster was being unloaded at a curbside and there was nothing to do but wait till it was set on the street. I started doing all those city things: looking at my watch, tapping my foot, feeling angry at no one in particular. And then I noticed that Dennis was mesmerized by the huge metal bin sliding off this enormous tractor, within an inch of the sidewalk. He was just so impressed by the size of the thing and the machinery. As the dumpster hit the curb, the tractor operator turned to us apologetically, but when he saw us, he only smiled. Dennis was applauding.

"The operator held up traffic for us as we crossed the street."

# PLAYGROUND LIFE

*T*he cloistered playground I take my daughter to is like *My Secret Garden*. It's always felt so private; there's a feeling of sharing among the mothers who go there. We don't even feel like we're in the city.

—Mary T., New York City

*T*he only time I ever talked to other parents of kids my son's age was on weekends...at the playground.

—Susan S., St. Paul, Minnesota

*I* go to the playground and I see my kid and other kids and how they play together and how much themselves they are, and I think, "Children are miracles!"

—Elke S., New York City

*G*od, it's *boring* in the playground.

—Margaret M., Chicago

Most city mothers begin taking their children to the playground as soon as the kids can sit up by themselves. We've seen mothers bring younger babies, but they seem so vulnerable—as if both they, as mothers, and their babies haven't quite hatched. The playground is a place for exposure to the social elements, to athletic experimentation; it's a testing ground and a place to learn—for both children and parents.

It is a place loaded with possibilities: for learning socialization, for increasing and improving motor skills, for learning independence, and for taking risks; it is also a place that nurtures feelings of competition, sometimes between parents, as well as feelings of isolation and boredom. How we respond to being in the playground with our children depends a lot on who we are and what our own playground experiences have been as children. We may go to the playground for the first time with no expectations at all and wind up loving it because it brings back all sorts of pleasant recollections, or we may look forward to spending time playing with our children outdoors but find the playground too confining. If we love being in the playground, we may feel guilty for just hanging out with our kids in the sand all day; if we hate it, we may feel guilty for not wanting to play with our kids in an environment they enjoy. But no matter which way we feel about it, there is always the potential to make almost any playground experience a learning, fruitful one. We might as well. For city parents and kids, without back yards or open fields, the playground experience is an inevitable one.

And an important one. Environmental psychologist Roger Hart, who specializes in the study of children's environments, says that a playground, especially a city playground, provides a place where a child can take risks and feel adventurous in a way that isn't dangerous to him. Hart feels, though, that in U.S. cities, where playgrounds are made of steel, concrete, and wood, they can become dangerous if they are exciting. For the younger child, supervised by a parent, the danger is a problem in that it requires more vigilant supervision, thoughtfulness, and diplomacy about how to limit risk-taking while encouraging a sense of freedom and accomplishment. It's important to decide for yourself what looks safe for your child and what doesn't. Check out playground equipment *before* your child

33

gets to it to make sure it's in good repair (see the box "Playground Safety"). If some equipment seems too advanced for your child, you may find yourself in the position of helping him or her *not* to do something, says Dr. Elaine Heffner. "You can say, 'I really can't handle that; it's too high for me.' It's good for kids to know you can't do everything. If you follow that with, 'But I think *you're* going to learn how to do it,' you are helping your child in another way: You are pointing out a separation between you. It is very important for a toddler and for you, too, to recognize that your child is not an extension of you."

---

## PLAYGROUND SAFETY

The U.S. Consumer Product Safety Commission estimates that, in one year, 118,000 playground equipment–related injuries received hospital emergency room treatment. Most injuries occur to children under ten years old. Falls from slides and climbing equipment are the most frequent hazard. But there are things the CPSC recommends that you can look for and things you can do to help minimize playground accidents.

Be sure equipment is on a soft ground surface: sand, rubber matting, or grass. It should be at least six feet from fences, walkways, walls, and other play areas. Legs should be set in concrete below ground level to prevent a tripping hazard. Slides should be in shaded areas to prevent burns; the landing pits in front of slides should be constructed from sand, tanbark, or similar materials to make coming off slides easier for younger, smaller kids. If there are seesaws in your playground—newer playgrounds often don't have them because they are now considered dangerous—a block placed under each end will prevent children from catching their feet if the board descends too rapidly.

Maintenance checks should be made at the beginning of the play season and at least every two weeks thereafter. Although the city should check and tighten any loose nuts, bolts, or hooks on a regular basis, parents should get used to checking this sort of thing in case it isn't done consistently. Apply tape over protruding screws or bolts and over sharp or rough edges—particularly on swing seats and on the edges of slides. Make sure rusted parts and worn ropes are replaced and that moving metal parts are oiled regularly. Rusted metal tubing should be sanded and repainted with unleaded paint, and wooden equipment should be sanded if it's rough.

Adapted from *Play Happy, Play Safely,* a U.S. Consumer Product Safety Commission pamphlet.

If you find that your kid has gotten to the top of a steep ladder or a slide and is afraid to come down—a very common reaction—it's best to try to talk him down. The feeling your child will get from doing something successfully he thought he couldn't do will be much more satisfying than the feeling he will get from doing something he knows he can do. From the former experience he will become aware of his abilities and therefore be able to use what he's learned. Making the fearful experience a learning experience is your first objective. You want to acknowledge your child's fear while showing him that he can overcome it himself; you want to punctuate your help with encouragement.

# WATCH OUT FOR THE NINE MAJOR PLAYGROUND EQUIPMENT DANGERS:

*Adapted from *Play Happy, Play Safely,* a U.S. Consumer Product Safety Commission pamphlet.

### Inadequate Spacing

Install the set a minimum of six feet away from fences, building walls, walkways, and other play areas, such as sandboxes.

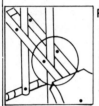

### Pinch-Crush Parts

Moving parts, particularly on gliders and seesaws, can pinch or crush fingers.

### Exposed Screws and Bolts

Most sets include protective caps to cover screws and bolts. When protective caps are not included, tape over all exposed screws and bolts, even those that appear to be out of the child's reach.

### Rings

Swinging exercise rings with a diameter between five and ten inches can entrap a child's head. Remove such rings and discard them so children will not find and play with them.

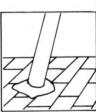

### Hard Surfaces

Do not install play equipment over hard surfaces such as concrete, brick, blacktop, or cinders. Grass or sand is better.

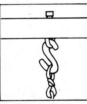

### S Hooks

Open-ended hooks, especially the *S* hooks on swings, which can catch skin or clothing, should be avoided. If a set has such hooks, pinch in the ends tightly with a pair of pliers.

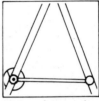

### Sharp Edges

Some sets have sharp edges or points where the parts fit together. Cover these areas with heavy tape and inspect the taped areas regularly for weather damage.

### Hard, Heavy Swing Seats

can strike a dangerous blow. Choose a swing set with lightweight seats or purchase such seats separately and replace the hard seats. Metal seats should have smooth, rolled edges.

### Improper Anchoring

Legs can be set in concrete for stability. All types of anchoring devices should be placed below ground level to avoid a tripping hazard.

## LEARNING TO LOVE THE PLAYGROUND

Those of us who enjoy spending time with our children in the playground like it because we like watching and helping our kids in physical and imaginative play, and we enjoy our own and our children's socializing. "On the days when I remembered that I wasn't in the playground just to keep Niva from killing herself, or some other kid, but instead to help her master her body and learn to enjoy other people, I had a real sense of accomplishment," says Bonnie. "With my first child, I went to the playground and sat there and gossiped and felt kind of useless at the end of the day, as if I'd wasted the afternoon. But when I feel I've taken advantage of lots of opportunities—okay, maybe just one or two a day, even—I feel like Niva and I are both growing. You know, it's being good to myself, really; it's taking my job as a parent seriously."

Of the mothers we spoke to who don't enjoy the playground, many said they feel socially excluded and bored. "The women in my neighborhood's two playgrounds are cliquish and cold," says one mother, a part-time music teacher. "I've never met anyone I'd want to establish a relationship with." If you do find socializing difficult, you can think of your own social difficulties as a metaphor for what the children are experiencing in the playground, says Dr. Heffner. With our adult social skills, we still sometimes find it uncomfortable. Our kids are just learning most of the social skills we take for granted.

"I don't love the playground," says Roz, "but I find 'play dates' even more tiresome than going to the park. At least in the playground I'm on neutral territory and I don't feel pressured to chat. I can read the paper, play with my kid, and leave whenever I want to without having to make excuses."

## HOW TO BE A SUCCESSFUL REF

When difficult situations between children arise, Laurie, a mother of three, found that approaching them as learning experiences often gave her a feeling of equanimity rather than irritation toward her own children and other people's. "Let's face it," she says, "when a kid throws sand in my kid's face, the first thing I want to do is pull the kid's hair out. But if I try to figure out what both kids are feeling, *I* always wind up feeling much better about it."

"I used to become so calm," says Elke, "when Alex did something irritating in the sandbox. I was afraid the other mothers would think I was this termagant woman with this horrible child, and I tried to compensate by being overly patient. It nearly killed me." Elke admits that she was very sensitive to the fact that people were making judgments about her son's and her own behavior. We've all done it—"Andrew is a bully, Jess is too passive, Eric is a wimp because he won't defend himself." But labeling kids is unconstructive; we do it instead of looking at what the child is having a hard time with. Says Dr. Heffner, "You wouldn't say, if your child is having a hard time with numbers, 'Boy is he stupid!' You would say, 'I wonder why he can't get it and how I can help him?'"

"We are very focused on cognitive learning nowadays," Dr. Heffner continues. "Parents are very clear about children not born knowing colors and numbers and the alphabet. But we are less clear about the fact that dealing with social encounters is another kind of learning. And that kind of learning takes even longer to sink in because there are a lot of feelings involved. There's a lot of emotion when somebody grabs your shovel."

So what's the best way to deal with unpleasant behavior or a confrontation between two young kids? First, wait and see what the children do by themselves. Clarify for the kids what happened—sometimes a young child doesn't even know what's happened—and offer some solutions. You can ask if the child wants to share his toy or ask for it back. What you'll be doing is taking the opportunity to teach different values to your child, says Dr. Heffner. Maybe you want to teach your son about ownership one day, or brotherhood another day. You'll have to be flexible about your agenda to take into consideration your child's feelings on any particular day, but your child will be exposed to lots of different situations and you will find plenty of opportunities to teach him different values.

## PLAYGROUND POTENTIALS

Most of the mothers we spoke to say they enjoy themselves more and think their kids do, too, when there are organized activities in the playground. "There's a folksinger who comes once a week to a playground I go to in the summer," says one mother, "and the kids are wild for her. She actually has my sons doing *folk dances*. I feel they're learning something—not just chasing each other around the sandbox."

If you're interested in bringing activities to the playground you frequent, take a petition to your city's parks and recreation department through your local community board (or your local governmental body). If you want faster results and you're more ambitious, try to get together a few parents to organize activities such as storytelling (which any parent can do), watercolor painting, or clay modeling. If you're nostalgic, teach a group of kids to play hopscotch, red light, or kick the can. The playground is one area of the city that's there just for you and your kids; take advantage of it creatively.

It's great if your city offers organized programs in the playground, but if it doesn't, parents taking the initiative can be just as successful. One playgroup formed by four mothers and their kids collected about $5 a month from each family for paints and books. When they got to know each other well, two mothers of the group assumed an on-duty day once a week for a few hours in the playground so that the other two could have some time to themselves. They supplemented the rather predictable playground equipment with playthings they brought on their own: an inflatable mattress the kids loved to roll around on and drag each other around on in the sand, and a thick rope for tug-of-war. When winter necessitated moving inside, the playgroup located a vacant room in an apartment building nearby and moved the whole thing indoors.

Anthony Procaccino, director of the Arts and Special Activities Division of the Cincinnati Recreation Commission, says that an effort to organize almost always improves the effectiveness of playgrounds. Ninety-five percent of the success in Cincinnati's playgrounds is due to organization, he says. And, he points out, if you and your children are pleased with the way your playground looks, you'll enjoy it more—which is a good reason to adopt your neighborhood playground. Parents who are involved in maintenance and activities say they've not only enjoyed a more pleasant playground but have also felt a strong sense of community and feeling of pride in "their park."

Psychologist Roger Hart emphasizes that "children like to use the environment not just as a container in which to play but as a set of props through which to play." Most playgrounds in our cities, he says, provide the stage, but not the props. That's why you, and probably most other mothers you see on your way to the playground, are laden with what Hart calls "loose parts"—objects kids can use as props in symbolic and imaginary play. The loose parts we bring for toddlers—

dump trucks, empty yogurt cartons, measuring spoons—are all a crucial part of our children's play. If you find, as we did, that your child is more interested in playing with other children's toys at the playground, you might try taking up a collection among parents for inexpensive objects (such as plastic kitchen utensils) that the kids can use in the sandbox and set them out for all the kids below a certain age. If there's water available, you can enhance water play by bringing containers with a few or many holes poked through the bottoms.

If you're looking to improve your playground, there are several elements you'll want to be aware of. According to Edmund Schubert, director of design for the New York City Parks and Recreation Department, the best playground is one that attracts people of all ages; it's integrated into the city neighborhood in such a way that it's off the streets but it isn't isolated from all street activity; there's plenty of opportunity for water play, sand play (although in New York City, the parks department does not like to use sand because of animal feces, broken glass, and other potential maintenance problems), and equipment that encourages both fine and gross motor skills. There ought to be areas where adults can sit comfortably to watch their children and talk to each other, a separate area for equipment that gives motion—such as swings and ropes—and climbing apparatus. Shade trees or a shade structure should allow relief from the sun over most of the area except for the water. Last, but importantly, the playground should attract lots of children of different ages and abilities (including handicapped kids).

A July 1986 *New York Times* survey found that playground attendants had a strong positive impact on the conditions of New York City's playgrounds. If you're lucky enough to have a playground staffed by teens in your neighborhood, so much the better: As Colin Ward points out in *The Child in the City* (New York: Pantheon, 1978): "There is a time-honored but grossly neglected educational adage: Each one teach one. This implies firstly that children learn best from older children, and secondly that teaching other children is itself a learning experience."

"In the city, especially," says Roger Hart, "it's more difficult for a child to learn somehow to develop a culture of his own, independent of his parents." Children have traditionally done that, he says, in the world of play. "They should have a place to play where they can go independently," he says, "away from their parents' watchful eyes and return to their parents for help when they need it." Most likely, the playground will be the first neutral place your city kid has for that experience.

# CHOICES IN CHILD CARE: BESIDES YOU, WHO?

*W*hat kind of effect is my being at work all day—away from my daughter—going to have on her?

—Susan P., New York City

*W*orried about a housekeeper raising your child? What are you worried about? Are you there in the morning? At night? On weekends? Did you hire a stable, responsible, loving person? Worried? What are you, nuts?

—Gail M., Philadelphia, psychologist and mother of two

*T*he child-care problem in this country is part of a larger indifference to ensuring the future of our children as a society. We have no national family policy. What our society is saying to parents is, "Child care is your personal problem."

—Barbara Reisman, mother of two and executive director of the Child Care Action Campaign

As any city parent knows, this particular personal problem profoundly shapes our lives and influences how we feel. One city mother put it this way: "When I feel confident about how my kids are being cared for, I feel an incredible freedom. When I have doubts about it, it casts a pall over every other area of my life."

There are no federal regulations for child-care services, and state regulations vary. Licensing, if properly enforced, can help set standards and establish channels of communication for child-care providers, but it does not guarantee good quality care.

What does this mean for the city parent? For one thing, like parents everywhere, you are totally responsible for your child-care decision. You must locate the care giver or the care-giving situation, must do the interviewing, check the situation against your own criteria, draw up any contracts, and keep a vigilant eye on what is happening with your child while in the care giver's domain.

For city parents, living space can be a child-care concern. Even for those with enough money to hire a full-time, in-home care giver, a relatively small apartment may be too confining for a toddler or preschooler. Exposure to other children is sometimes difficult to arrange, and so a city parent might opt for a center-based or group care for an older toddler rather than a full-time care giver. Safety is another important consideration. Because of city traffic and the variety of people their kids are exposed to, city parents are exquisitely aware that whoever cares for their children must be vigilant.

---

## THE WORKING MOTHER'S DILEMMA

Although the poor are hardest hit by the child-care crisis in this country, middle-class parents feel it, too. For us, finding good care is difficult and often expensive, and our choices about how we are going to live with our children are limited. We are often forced to decide between giving up a much-needed salary to stay home with our kids, or feeling that we aren't with our kids enough because for whatever reason—financial or not—we've had to return to work.

For those of us who do work outside the home, the big question is, What is my being away from my child all day doing to him?

Ellen Galinsky, director of Work and Family Life Studies at Bank Street College in New York City, says that the

---

mere fact that you work is *not* what affects your child.*
The impact of your working depends upon the conditions
of your job and of your family life. She names four factors she thinks can make a positive or negative difference
for your child:

1 Your own and/or your family's attitude toward your
  working. If the attitude is positive, then your family
  will more likely feel a sense of pride and closeness
  about it.
2 The conditions of your job: Stresses on the job can be
  brought home and affect your children.
3 Other stressful events within the family. Marital problems plus job stress adds up to a lot of stress on the
  children. But taking steps to resolve the problems can
  reduce the impact.
4 The quality of the care your child is getting. The re-
  sponsiveness of the care giver to your child's needs,
  the consistency of the care, the discipline style of the
  care giver, and the language development the care
  giver stimulates are all important.

*From the forthcoming *Family Matters and the Preschool Years*, by Ellen
Galinsky and Judy David (New York: Times Books, 1988), adapted in
*Childcare Information Exchange* 48 (March 1986): 19–23.

## THE OPTIONS

The Child Care Action Campaign (a national child-care advo-
cacy group based in New York City) telescopes child-care
choices into two categories: in-family care and community
care. According to its statistics, in-family care is used by more
than half of all working parents (but the city parents we spoke
to did not use in-family care more than any other kind of care).
According to the CCAC, in-family care consists of arranging

work hours so that one parent is always home; using a relative, a close friend, or an older sibling; or combinations of these arrangements. Community care comprises five options: First there's *in-home care*, with a nanny or a babysitter coming to the child's home. This is an expensive solution for full-time care, but it's cost effective if you have more than one preschool-age child. Less expensive are *shared care*, with several families hiring someone to care for all their children in one of their homes; *family day care*, with children being cared for in the home of the care giver, and *group family day care*, with more children cared for by two providers in one of the provider's homes. Finally, there are *day-care centers*, full-day or part-day programs, serving larger groups of children and not located in a private home.

Dr. Bryna Siegel-Gorelick points out in her excellent book, *The Working Parents' Guide to Child Care* (Boston: Little, Brown, 1983), the four major topics you must consider when choosing your child-care option are location, flexibility, cost, and availability of the necessary child-related paraphernalia.

## IN-HOME CARE GIVERS
### BABYSITTERS, NANNIES, AND HOUSEKEEPERS

Although it's pretty easy to find women who would like work as live-out, full-time care givers in any city that is host to a service class of new immigrants who lack training and who haven't got U.S. high school diplomas, finding the person who is just right for you and your family (and training her) is not easy at all. But it is possible. Many of these people have gone through their native country's educational systems and are smart, patient, and love kids.

Full-time care givers are covered by the minimum wage law, but most earn at least $5 an hour and the wages are subject to social security tax, as well as liability and unemployment compensation. Having a full-time, in-home care giver is pricey, but the benefits can be great; and if you're a working couple, this is the only option that guarantees you won't lose time at work if your child gets sick (although if she gets sick, you'll need a backup). You are basically hiring a full-time, stay-at-home housewife/mother.*

We're going to refer to in-home caregivers as housekeepers, since that was the most commonly used word in our interviews, but we note the misnomer. Obviously, it's one thing to take care of a house and a very different thing to take care of a child. Whatever you choose to call the person who takes care of your children and keeps your house in order, it is critical that she clearly understands her work priorities.

The quickest, easiest, and most expensive way to find a housekeeper or a babysitter is to call an agency that specializes in child care and screens applicants. You will have to pay a fee of about two weeks of the employee's salary. If the housekeeper you want to hire doesn't have a work permit, it is your responsibility to sponsor her; some agencies can help make necessary arrangements. Advertising in a local or ethnic paper may bring a more manageable number of responses than if you advertise in a large circulation newspaper. (One New York mother who advertised in the *Irish Echo* got over fifty calls in a week, but another who advertised in the *Times* got, she says, at least three hundred calls and though she had specified hours appropriate to phone, it seemed no one saw that part of her ad). Finding someone by word-of-mouth is great, but even if

---

*In addition, under the new Immigration Reform and Control Act, it is unlawful to hire aliens who lack authorization to work in the United States. To verify the employment eligibility of your housekeeper, you should request documentation (such as a U.S. passport, a Certification of United States Citizenship, a Certificate of Naturalization, or an Alien Registration Receipt Card) that establishes her identity and her eligibility to work.

you have lots of contacts, it's sometimes slow. A word-of-mouth prospect at least comes recommended by friends or friends of friends.

### The Interview

You should conduct two interviews with your prospective housekeeper. The first is the screening or telephone interview, during which you can find out how much experience she has had with children and if her work goals coincide with your needs. Dr. Siegel-Gorelick gives great advice about how to conduct what she calls an open-ended interview in your home in order to get at a potential housekeeper's values and attitudes about child rearing: Ask first how the housekeeper feels about her own children or the children she has taken care of. Some questions to ask: What would you say to my child if he started crying for me while I wasn't here? How do you feel about disciplining a child? Why do you want to take care of children? What is it you like about kids? What did you like and dislike about the people you worked for previously?

Listen closely to the emotional tone the housekeeper uses when talking about her own kids or her former charges and, if she wants to, let her continue talking about one issue (the more she talks about it the less superficial she's likely to be on the subject). Siegel-Gorelick also suggests asking the housekeeper about hypothetical situations; it may make her feel more comfortable, she says, and remind her of things that really did happen in her last job and how she handled them.

On the second in-person interview you can present a written list of the housekeeper's duties, along with rules about safety in the home and outside, as well as go over the salary. If you like her and you see that your child likes her—or, depending upon his age, is not put off by her—and you think you would like to hire her, you can show her around your apartment. Depending upon your means, you may be able to do this without getting up, but in any case it's important that she see your place in order for her to decide if she wants to take the job, especially if you expect her to keep house as well as to care for your child.

## The Relationship

The intricacies of the housekeeper/parent/child relationship can be surprising. "It never occurred to me that it would be so complicated," one new mother told us. But why shouldn't it be? You hire a relative stranger to care for one of the people you care most about. You may discover that you are suddenly sharply ambivalent about returning to work after your child's birth and have complicated feelings about leaving him in someone else's care. And that's only a fourth of the picture. You are also influenced by how the caregiver feels, as well as your child's and your husband's reactions. So when you think you need to feel in-charge and authoritative, you may wind up feeling vulnerable instead.

For many of us, a large part of our choice to live in a city has to do with our careers; when children arrive, sometimes bringing with them a reexamination of our values, we begin to feel ambivalent about our work and child-care choices. But, as one mother pointed out, when she was able to accept that she will probably always feel ambivalent about leaving her daughter in someone else's care, she felt tremendously relieved.

---

### HOUSEKEEPER SAFETY

When you're training someone to care for your child in your own home and expect her to take your child to the park and on errands, it's best to spend a week at home, if

CHOICES IN CHILD CARE: BESIDES YOU, WHO?

you can, to show her the ropes and to reduce your involvement gradually.

Make sure the housekeeper knows where the first-aid materials are and that she knows the evacuation procedure in case of a fire. List important telephone numbers next to the telephone, and make it clear whom she should call first in an emergency. "Penelope Leach's *Your Baby and Child* is my bible," said one mother, who works full time. "I bought an extra copy and gave it to my housekeeper. 'Read this book,' I told her. 'I believe in it.' I know she uses it because on more than one occasion when I've expressed bafflement at something, my four-year-old has said to me, 'Let's look it up in Penelope Leach!' "

The many parents we spoke to who were able to preserve the delicate balance of control and respect, of intimacy and professionalism, that make up the housekeeper/employer relationship, offered these pieces of advice:

- **Don't be paralyzed by insecurities.** The bottom line in having a successful relationship with a housekeeper is coming to terms with your decision to hire one. If you feel that you don't deserve help or you need to feel that no one can do the job of taking care of your kids better than you, you will never be satisfied with anyone you hire. As one psychologist says, "Children need to be loved, cared for, and taken seriously. I don't worry about stimulation. There's plenty of stimulation in that."
- **Be warm and kind, fair and human.** But you must never forget that you are in an employer/employee relationship, and that you are the boss. You may not feel like a boss the day your newborn slips out of your hands in the bath or

51

the day you have a screaming fight with your teenaged daughter, so this can be hard. Although it's hard to translate managerial skills you've learned on the job over to your relationship with your housekeeper, since you share many intimacies, it's important to be organized, to give feedback, to schedule specific times to talk, and to honor your commitments the same way you would with a co-worker. The more integrated your housekeeper becomes into the family, the more confusing it is. Your relationship needs constant evaluation and care.

- Be sure your housekeeper is willing to share your general approach to childrearing. She does not have to initiate it, but she does have to understand it. Agonizing over the differences in your values will eventually bring you to this conclusion (assuming you've hired a moral person): There's a way the housekeeper does things and there's a way you do things, and your kid is probably going to opt for the way you do things. Your kids may be getting mixed messages from you and your housekeeper. As long as both are benign and caring, it probably doesn't matter. It's important to avoid the pitfall of competing for, rather than sharing, a small child's care, according to Dr. T. Berry Brazelton, in *Toddlers and Parents* (New York: Delacorte, 1974).
- When a housekeeper does not speak English with the same fluency as you do, you need to consider two things: Can she express her sense of humor in English so that your child can understand it? And can she negotiate a tight situation in more than one way so that she is not, when trying to get your child to do something, only saying the same thing over and over, louder and louder? Can she stimulate language development in your child either in her native tongue or yours?

- Get to know people in common. It's a great way to tell how things are going with your housekeeper and your kids when you're not around. If you both know some of the people where your kids spend time (the park, a play-group), you can take advantage of that. Then, too, learning to trust a housekeeper comes from watching her time and time again resolve small emergencies satisfactorily.
- Keep your perspective. One reason the housekeeper/employer relationship is tough is that you are paying a stranger to love your child. If she really does love your child, how can you ever feel that you've paid her enough? Develop a style of discussing things together, asking questions, chatting, talking about your child every day, so that when you have to talk to each other about something very important, it won't be so difficult.
- Ask for suggestions; you don't necessarily have to capitulate, but it's good to involve your housekeeper in your child-rearing decisions.
- Even though you may feel you pay your housekeeper enough for you to have flexibility as a perk, try not to overdo the times you change plans that affect her or say, "I'll take over now." Your housekeeper needs some autonomy, too. Remember also, that sometimes a housekeeper might need a day off or a few hours away from her work. Don't you? Recognize this need, and if it's at all possible, suggest it and allow for it.
- Don't rely on your housekeeper for things that you could do yourself. You will begin to feel beholden to her in an unhealthy way.
- When your housekeeper leaves, try to help your child express grief, if it's appropriate. Accept the child's feelings, and talk about them a lot. Look at pictures of your child and the housekeeper, or borrow a video camera and tape

her before she leaves. Draw pictures of her with your child. Phone her.

Losing a housekeeper is a controllable thing most of the time, so you try to avoid it. But worse things happen. Kids are resilient.

## FAMILY DAY CARE*

Family day care is home-based child care, provided by a woman in her own home, usually for six or fewer children. Most often, at least one of the children is the caretaker's. According to the CCAC, more than 1.5 million women in the United States provide home-based care to more than 5 million children—70 percent of the children in full-time care. The benefits of home-based care are, first of all, providing your child is cared for in your own neighborhood, there's no transportation problem. Secondly, it costs less than an at-home care giver, (though you could expect to pay as much as $125 to $150 a week for full-time care,) and often less than center-based care. Third, your child is exposed to other children and can enjoy the benefits of being in a home. The ratio of care givers to children is usually one to three. Furthermore, a family day-care provider will probably be flexible enough to meet your occasional special needs, and you may be able to arrange to pay only when your child is cared for, so you don't have to worry about taking your child out of care for a week and losing money.

The main problem with family day care is the same one you'd have if you hired a full-time housekeeper: If the care giver gets sick and can't work, you're up the creek unless you

*This information is adapted from the Child Care Action Campaign.

have a backup. Locating family day care might also be somewhat difficult. The CCAC suggests calling your local department of health and human services, checking the phone book for family day-care associations, child-care resource and referral services, or talking to people at child-care centers. You can also check with Y's, schools, community groups, bulletin boards, and newspapers, and, if possible, spend a few days at the playground. In most neighborhoods you'll see the same faces there day after day, and if you don't actually see any day-care providers, you will at least be able to ask other mothers who they know.

The Child Care Action Campaign offers these guidelines for selecting a family day care home:

- Is the home clean? Safe? Roomy enough to accommodate the number of children under care?
- Do other children in the home seem happy and involved enough in an activity so that they are not unduly distracted by you when you visit?
- Do you instinctively feel you can trust the provider? Has she had any training in child care?
- Is there sufficient play equipment to provide activities for all the children? Is there outdoor space somewhere in the neighborhood, and are there arrangements for children to be out of doors for part of the day?
- Is there an emergency number posted so that in case of need a doctor can be reached?
- Does the provider welcome visits from parents?
- Is the home licensed or registered?
- Are the children all around the same age?

After your child has been in the home for several weeks, consider:

- Is she happy?
- Does she look forward to going to the family day-care home?
- Is there any significant negative change in the child's behavior, such as withdrawal or tantrums, that should be discussed with the provider?

Because there is little regulation of family day care, you as a parent must be vigilant about your choice. That means that, among other things, no matter how uncomfortable it makes you, you've got to check out the provider's home thoroughly.

## DAY-CARE CENTERS

One working mother who was happy with her full-time housekeeper told us, "Even though I know my kids are doing well with our housekeeper, I'd advise parents to consider day care before automatically choosing a housekeeper, even if they can afford it. For one thing, you don't have to deal with the complex relationship you inevitably develop with a full-time care giver or housekeeper, and, for another, certain things that can become a big deal when you're going it alone just aren't, when your kids are around other kids—toilet training, for example."

Studies show that good day-care centers have a positive effect on children. But quality is essential, and it is crucial that you know what kind of care your child is getting. The CCAC offers these guidelines for selecting a quality day-care center:

- Small groups work best. The ratio of provider to children should be high.

- The training of the care giver is important. Training in child development or early childhood education affects the quality of care.
- Continuity of relationships is important to children. Moving from center to center or a high turnover at one center is not good.
- The design of the environment is important. Children need to feel competent, and they need to engage in activities in small groups. Well-trained staff members set up the space and the equipment so that these needs are met.
- A cooperative relationship between parents and staff is essential.
- Basic health and safety, of course, are also essential.
- The match of program to a child's needs is important. Different children thrive in different types of programs. You'll know what's best for your child.
- The quality of the administration of the day-care center will have a major effect on the quality of the program for children and its effects on children.

If you are both working parents, a great benefit of day care is that if the care giver is sick, there will always be a substitute, so you never have to worry about missing work. (On the other hand, just as when your child is enrolled in school, your child will be more likely to get sick because of exposure to many other children.) Other benefits of day care centers: They offer your child stimulation and socialization; and they cost less than in-home care. According to Child Care, Inc., a resource and referral service in New York City, full-day private day-care centers charge from about $150 to $190 a week. A couple of drawbacks: Your child might not be the kind who thrives, at a young age, among many other children; and a full day of day care might be a lot for your child to handle.

## How to Choose a Day-Care Center

Again, because licensing doesn't ensure a day-care center's quality, you as a parent are responsible for checking it out. The Child Care Action Campaign offers these guidelines:

- Is the center licensed or registered? If your state does have licensing requirements, make sure the center is not breaking the law.
- Spend time in the center before and after your child is placed there. You should not only be welcomed but urged to visit as often as possible. You should be allowed to drop in without an appointment. Never leave your child in the care of anyone who tells you that parents are not allowed to visit as often as they like and whenever they can.
- Be sure that there are not too many children in the center and that each receives individual attention. You need to be satisfied that the provider will have the time and the energy to give your child the care and attention she needs.
- Are the teachers careful about hygiene and cleanliness? Caretakers should wash their hands frequently, especially after changing diapers. Older kids' hands should be washed before eating and after going to the bathroom. The environment should be reasonably clean and toys washed regularly.
- Be sure that there is no equipment or conditions in the center that can cause serious accidents or hurt your child. See if there is an emergency plan. Is it posted near the phone? Does everyone who cares for the children know exactly what to do in case of an emergency? Are there smoke detectors and fire extinguishers, as well as a plan for moving the children in case of a fire? Are there gates protecting kids from stairs? Is there a soft surface under climbing equipment? Are medicines stored out of the

58

reach of children? You are the inspector. If you don't see the answer to your questions, ask for it.

- Look for a variety of play equipment so that your child will have the chance to grow both physically and intellectually.
- Watch carefully to see if the children are busy and happy and if the adults are interested and loving. Put yourself in your child's place. Would you have wanted to be with these people when you were little?
- Be sure that the staff of your child-care center arranges for you to meet parents of the other children. If your kid is unhappy, or you feel that there are problems, you can talk to other parents and find out if your child's problems are common ones. It's also a good sign if the center is not protecting itself from parent solidarity. If you're feeling isolated because you don't know many other people with kids, this is obviously a good place to start meeting them.

---

### DAY CARE SAFETY

Whether you take your child to a day-care center or to family day care, be sure that these basic safety precautions are followed:

- There are strict provisions for the safe arrival and departure of children;
- There is an enclosed, protected outdoor play area;
- There is cushioning material under playground equipment;
- There are safety gates on stairs;
- All unused electrical outlets are covered;
- Medicines, cleaning supplies, and other potentially dangerous substances are stored off the floor in a locked cabinet;

- The indoor area and toys are cleaned and washed regularly;
- The staff washes their hands before feeding and after diapering;
- The staff knows and practices emergency evacuation procedures.

## SEPARATION ANXIETY: YOURS AND YOUR CHILD'S

*"If he doesn't stop crying in two weeks, I'm pulling him out."*
*"If I don't stop crying in two weeks, I'm pulling him out."*

Dr. Bryna Siegel-Gorelick in *The Working Parents' Guide to Child Care,* gives sound advice about how to adjust, yourself, and how to help your child adjust to day care. She points out that parental attitudes about departure and separation do influence how a child feels about those things, so it helps to know why you feel the way you do. If you can talk about your anxiety with another adult and name your fears to someone you trust to understand them, you might feel less uncomfortable. "I thought I would relish my freedom," one mother told us. "Instead I felt this terrible loss when my daughter started day care. The bottom line was that I didn't like leaving her with people who didn't love her as much as I did. It sounds unreasonable, and it is, but that's how I felt. It really wasn't until I began to see my daughter thriving in her day-care situation that I began to feel better about it."

If you see that you really have a problem leaving your child, try to get your spouse to be the last to leave the house, whether you have a full-time housekeeper or babysitter coming in or you're dropping off your child at a care-giving post.

Developing a ritual for separation, just like a bedtime ritual, eases the transition.

Siegel-Gorelick offers advice about how to help your child adjust:

- Try several one- to two-hour "warm-up" separations beforehand (useful with five- to ten-month-olds who can see that you're leaving but don't understand you yet when you say you will return.)
- Introduce him to other children, but don't force interaction between your child and another.
- Encourage him to explore on his own. Don't develop an activity for him that involves you too much.
- Stay tuned in to his activities. Don't stand around and chat with the care giver a lot.
- Don't hold or physically restrict him too much, but stay low to the floor and available.
- Try to get him involved in toys.
- Don't act like the teacher, playing with other children.
- Give your child a task to do when you're ready to leave. ("Play with the Tinker Toys—build me a house.")
- Always say good-bye, no matter what age your child is, but make your leave-taking brief.
- When you return for your child, don't be surprised if he acts angry at you; it's normal. If you respond to his anger with patience and love, he'll get over it.
- Let your child take the lead in his method of releasing tension at the end of the day. You know how to unwind. Your child doesn't. He may seem more active than usual when he first sees you again, or he may get quiet and cranky. Encourage your child to communicate and to describe what he's been doing.
- Remember, for both your sakes, that loving your child can

be demonstrated in ways that don't include being together twenty-four hours a day.

## CARE FOR SCHOOL-AGE CHILDREN

Children between the ages of five and about fifteen also need care before or after school, during school vacations, and on holidays when their parents must work. Some family day-care providers accept school-age children, and there are programs as well in some Y's and at many public and private schools and day care centers. The CCAC advises that the cost for a school-age child program can run from $15 to $20 a week and up.

## HOW TO START A BABYSITTING CO-OP

If you don't relish the idea of leaving your child with a stranger for the evening or paying someone $5 or more an hour for watching television while your baby sleeps, you might want to consider starting or joining a babysitting co-op. The point of a co-op is to allow you to trade your babysitting services with another parent's in your neighborhood. No money is involved.

One of the co-ops in the Chelsea section of New York City began with about twenty-five members (which the current members consider a good number), but a co-op can work with fewer. Members often meet each other in the playground or a play-group, or get to know each other in other parent/child-related activities. Co-op meetings are held once or twice a year; the officers are volunteers whose positions are rotated every four to six months. In the Chelsea co-op there is a president and a secretary, who records points given for babysitting. There is usually a membership list, which includes names, addresses, phone numbers, and availability for babysitting, as well as names and ages of kids.

The Chelsea co-op uses a point system to keep track of services: four points are granted for an hour of sitting; six points an hour after midnight; and six an hour for two kids if they are both awake. Parents' Resources, Inc., in New York City, reports that some co-ops use "currency" rather than points— pennies painted with red nail polish, for example, each worth a half hour of babysitting. Each family gets forty pennies, worth twenty hours, upon entering the co-op. Trust among members usually prevents parents from using up their twenty hours and then leaving the co-op.

Co-ops develop a list of rules, followed religiously or not at all depending on the type of people in the group. Parents' Resources reports the most basic rules include:

- No one is obligated to accept any given assignment; but each member family must contribute equal sitting time.
- Babysitting is done in the home of the sitter during the day and at the home of the child at night.
- If the sitter cancels within twenty-four hours of the obligation, he is required to find a replacement from within the co-op or to pay for a babysitter (and good luck finding one, too). If the parents cancel within twenty-four hours, they are required to pay the babysitter for one hour's worth of sitting. In the Chelsea co-op, cancelations are dealt with by penalty points at the discretion of the inconvenienced member. Members are also required to give the sitter the time they will be returning and to phone the sitter within a half hour of that time if they will be late.

The disadvantages of participating in a co-op are pretty obvious: If you work a long day yourself, or if your spouse does, you probably won't much feel like taking care of someone else's kids when you get home. It may not be worth trading time if you'll be miserable every time you're called on to do your share. But a co-op can be a great advantage if you do have time, if you prefer having your kids watched by neighbors you are at least acquainted with, and/or you want to get to know the other parents and children in your neighborhood. And as one Chelsea mother said, "It's good to know that your kid is being cared for by another parent if something goes wrong. Experience does count."

## RESOURCE AND REFERRAL SERVICES

Child-care resource and referral services have different names, but according to the CCAC, they may:

- provide information about the facilities in your city, including centers, family day care, group homes, and other kinds of informal arrangements;
- know which programs have vacancies and have detailed information about each service;
- provide criteria for choosing the best arrangement for your child;
- help new facilities get started;
- try to improve quality in child-care facilities;
- provide parent education seminars.

For more information about resource and referral agencies in your area, send a self-addressed, stamped envelope with a request for information about your state to:

CHILD CARE ACTION CAMPAIGN
99 HUDSON STREET, ROOM 1233
NEW YORK, NEW YORK 10013

## ADVOCACY

As Barbara Reisman, executive director of the Child Care Action Campaign says, "Parents have an obligation to be advocates of child care as a public issue. As employers and employees they must recognize that it is an issue that requires corporate and political involvement."

For information about how you can help improve child care services, contact:

CHILD CARE ACTION CAMPAIGN
99 HUDSON STREET, ROOM 1233
NEW YORK, NEW YORK 10013

CHILDREN'S DEFENSE FUND,
CHILD CARE DIVISION
122 C STREET, NW
WASHINGTON, DC 20001

NATIONAL ASSOCIATION FOR THE EDUCATION
OF YOUNG CHILDREN
1834 CONNECTICUT AVENUE, NW
WASHINGTON, DC 20009-5786

NATIONAL ORGANIZATION FOR WOMEN
1401 NEW YORK AVENUE, NW, SUITE 800
WASHINGTON, DC 20005

# FIRST LESSONS: CHOOSING A NURSERY SCHOOL

*W*hen Jesse was two and a half, I knew it was time for him to go to school. Let me put it another way—when I was thirty and a half, I knew it was time for me to be alone a little more. But I felt guilty about my urgent desire to be free of Jesse—so I drove myself crazy until I found what was the most enriched, most opulent, most progressive nursery school in the city. Then I wasted half my time getting there, worried about the ridiculous price, felt like an idiot when I was just as tired after picking him up at noon as I'd have been if he'd stayed home. I sent my second kid to this very nice nursery school next to our building. It was just as good.

—Naomi L., Cleveland, mother of two

*I* chose a nursery school—a day-care center, really—because Evan's best friend was going there. And, since Evan's mom was my best friend, it made it easy for both of us to share dropoffs, pickups, and dates. The center was in the neighborhood; it was warm and friendly and well integrated—a very city environment. He loved it, but I worried because I had other friends who'd gotten their kids into nursery programs that were associated with prestigious grade schools. I actually thought —forgive me—would my kid ever catch up and get into a good college? Of course he did.

—Judy B., Brooklyn, New York

*T* he most important thing you do in nursery school is play and take naps. So I think a mother should ask the teachers if a kid can whisper during nap-time. If you can whisper, that probably means it was a nice nursery school. Good teachers are also important, but if you can whisper, that's one way to tell a good teacher.

—Steven S., San Francisco, a nursery school graduate

Parents everywhere worry about the quality of their children's education. But once parents in small towns and suburbs choose a home in a good school district, they have answered the basic question, What kind of education should my child have? City parents are faced with an entirely different set of circumstances. As soon as a city child is two or three, we must ask ourselves: What is my philosophy of education? Do I believe in public education or private? Do I believe in a structured school, a progressive school, a school with students from all classes and races, a school with social concerns, a religion-based school, an alternative school, a neighborhood school?

This is the first extraordinary fact of being a city parent: Each one of us chooses how to educate our own children. Each one of us must get to know what we believe in before we decide on what is a simpler matter in small towns and suburbs —where to send our three-year-old to school.

This situation results in an equally extraordinary fact: Each city kid is put on his *own* educational track. A five-year-old may be going to kindergarten and already bidding his first alma mater and first school friends adieu. A sixteen-year-old in a city like New York may very well have followed a unique path—a certain day care center, then nursery school, then private school, then public high school—that *no one* else in his grade, in the entire city, could match exactly.

There are clearly pros and cons to this situation, but they *are* the facts of city life simply because the city is not defined by its family life and structures but rather by its adult life. As a result, we city parents must gather—from here and there, from this school and that church, from this afterschool program and that set of friends—our own family community.

And yet if you feel continually faced with difficult choices, keep in mind the big picture: Like so many forms of city culture, the alternatives are excellent. You won't go wrong if you choose one hit show over another, a museum show over a stroll down gallery row, a small park to play in instead of a big one—*or* one good nursery school over another.

Creating your own educational system from a host of alternatives can be a pain in the neck, but it is an extraordinary opportunity. What follows is some basic information that we hope will help you with those choices.

## WHAT KIND OF NURSERY SCHOOL?

*Most* nursery schools are warm and friendly; have teachers, whatever their various styles, who love and relate well to little kids; have enough blocks and fingerpaints and unusual creative activities. It's the irrational personal requirements that can drive us crazy when we make our preschool decisions.

We look at a school and ask: Could this nursery school get my kid into a good college?

We look around the classroom and think: If this school is formal and restrictive about water and sand play, will my child grow up to be an uptight accountant?

We talk to our friends and wonder: Since Tracy looked at twelve nursery schools before making her choice and since, while her kids are gone every morning, she attends seminars in child development, am I a lazy parent?

Although lots of us tend to ask such questions, they are not going to help us choose a better nursery school. A city mother of a city toddler should visit and investigate recommended schools to find the answer to two basic questions and two questions only:

The first is: If you were three, would you want to be left here when your mom waved good-bye?

And the second, and equally important, is: Is this school going to make my life as a parent easier and happier, or harder and more stressful?

Every other question you ask should help to answer those two questions.

We recommend the following guidelines based on the interviews we conducted with dozens of mothers. The guidelines are listed in the order of importance most mothers assigned them, but feel free to reorder the list. Remember, it helps to be flexible.

1. • *Choose a neighborhood nursery school.* Most parents and experts suggest that the first thing you should look for is a neighborhood nursery school. There is nothing more pleasant than walking your child to school; meeting other parents and kids; and knowing that these kids and parents are close by—for after-school dates, for impromptu babysitting when you've got to be somewhere, and (last but not least important) for creating a sense of community for your whole family. Don't turn into a nursery-school commuter.

2. • *Look closely at the teachers.* Many parents worry first about a "philosophy" of a nursery school, but nothing will give you a greater sense of well-being than sitting in on a class or two or three to watch the teachers and their assistants in action, as well as meeting the head of the school. The fact is, many preschool teachers could teach in any school; they follow many philosophies and often do switch from school to school. Do you like the

teachers? Do the kids like them? Love them? Chances are, if both answers are yes, your child is in good hands.

3. • *Meet and talk to the other parents.* If *you* feel comfortable with the parent body and the setting, your child probably will. Remember—you'll be making friends there, too. In fact, if you look at the parents' faces and demeanor, you'll probably instinctively know a lot about the style and values of the school.

4. • *Determine whether the school has a philosophy you respect.* One city mother remembers visiting a Montessori school at the recommendation of a friend whose daughter adored the place. She sat in on a class with a very competent but formal teacher and left thinking of the Montessori method as too structured. Her friend was shocked and urged her to pay one more visit. She did, and this time she sat in on a different class, with a warm, motherly, easygoing teacher. This time she came back thinking the Montessori system was a relaxed, loving, *and* enriched environment.

Ultimately, we believe the philosophies of most nursery schools are primarily dependent on the teachers and on the director who sets the *mood* of the school and the morale for the teachers. Therefore the best way to determine that philosophy is to forget the school's label and observe how the staff actually carries out the following three basic goals of any nursery school.

*The first goal of nursery school is to help a three- or four-year-old successfully separate from his or her parents (and to help the parents separate from the child).*

Striking a balance between attachment and separation is one of the most difficult tasks of childhood and parenthood. One of the first places to practice is at nursery school. How does the school you're visiting handle and facilitate the process?

For example, when Diane had to leave her eldest son, John, at his nursery school, it was painfully difficult. "I stayed the first three mornings with all the other parents.... On the following morning, I dropped John off and, my heart in my mouth, started to leave when the other mothers did. Four kids started to scream and John was one of them, so four of us stayed in the waiting room for a while longer. Soon, three kids were still screaming. The next day two of us were in that anteroom. The next day, just my John was still crying. I was a mess. My heart was breaking. I was afraid my boss would get angry, and I felt I'd flunked parenthood. Why wasn't John as independent and secure as all those other kids? Luckily John's teacher reassured me that each kid handled the initial separation differently and asked me to be patient....I stayed in the classroom and then the anteroom and then the teachers' lounge farthest away from his class for almost two weeks. Finaly, one morning, John took my hand in his little fist and said, 'Mommy, see ya later.' We both enjoyed the rest of the day. And I'd grown to know and trust John's teacher."

Talk to parents who've made the break at the school you're considering. Talk to the staff and especially to the director. Is she comfortable with parents around? Sure, she likes kids, but does she like parents? Is she patient, intelligent, flexible? Remember, you're always asking two questions—is this school good for my kid, and is it good for me. A school that makes a parent feel successfully separated will probably be sensitive to making the children feel successful every day they're there.

*The second goal of nursery school is to help a toddler begin the "socialization" process*—what used to be called "working and playing well with others."

Observe the following to determine a nursery school or teacher's approach to socialization.

Does a teacher respect kids of different styles equally? Does the school help an aggressive kid master his aggression, and a more timid kid assert him or herself? As one teacher said, "By the end of the year, we try to get the child whose been 'following' all year to be

In nursery school, kids learn to separate from their parents and form rewarding friendships. (PHOTO BY TRUDE GLASSER)

able to lead if he wants, and the aggressive kid to feel more comfortable by himself, to even 'follow' others."

How does the school handle and respect kids of each gender? One mother told us that in her son's nursery school, the very sweet teacher was clearly more comfortable with girls than boys. Boys were constantly being reprimanded for being wild, for running, etc. Girls were constantly being praised. On the other hand, another mother emphasized that one of the things she loved about her nursery school was that the teacher encouraged the boys to play with dolls and costumes as well as to climb in the playground. And she encouraged the girls to climb and to play in the block corner. "It was great to see my daughter Jennifer play with those big wooden blocks, to build. True, she still didn't build what the boys were building—solar systems and buildings. She built split-level houses and little dress shops. But there was a sense of possibility at that place. I liked it."

Another way of comprehending the school's "socialization" techniques is to note how the school or the teacher handles conflicts. Drop in unannounced one day, then hang around and wait for a fight between two kids. (You won't have to wait long.) How does the teacher resolve it? Does she just separate the kids or does she discuss their behavior? Does she say, pragmatically, "My job is to keep kids from getting hurt here, so I don't allow hitting. I'm going to have to separate you two." Does she take the psychological approach, asking the "victim," "Why do you think Timmy was angry at you?" Or does she prefer the moral approach, telling Timmy, "Say you're sorry"?

Preschool society is precivilization, a wild kingdom,

and the teachers are the lion tamers, the imposers of an order—pragmatic, psychological, or moral. You should know which order or which combination you are most comfortable with.

If you're not comfortable, talk to the teacher and ask why she has chosen her particular approach. You might be convinced. These teachers *have* seen hundreds of kids.

But if you're not, remember that *you are your child's parent.* No one knows your child or the way you want her raised better than you do. Trust your gut instincts.

*The third goal of nursery school is to help your child to explore age-appropriate objects and activities by making them available to him or her.* Here it's important to consider what the school feels your child should be taught. Are academic, reading, and writing skills a priority, or are general knowledge and learning through play the primary educational aims?

Many parents are concerned that their toddler get a good academic start, but experts differ on what that means. Some, such as David Elkind, author of *The Hurried Child* (Reading, Mass.: Addison-Wesley, 1981) feel that little kids should not be rushed—that although knowledge is important, the preschooler pays a heavy price when academics are placed before emotional and social development. In fact, he says, "All the evidence indicates that children who have been taught to read early (as opposed to those who learned on their own) are no further ahead at nine or ten than children who learned to read later." He is therefore critical of nursery schools that have reading and writing sessions, stencils for copying letters, math flash cards, et cetera.

On the other hand, you may feel that your child's intellectual potential is untapped and she should begin to explore academics as early as six months old. Most nursery schools continue to be more Elkind-oriented— more traditional, emphasizing teaching through play. But because there is a stress on academics these days and because nursery school directors respond to parental pressure, many acknowledged that they are providing more reading and writing training in their programs than ever before.

Whatever your academic preferences, any good nursery school should, above all, be stimulating to all the senses of a child. Beware of a school that has stencils but no costume corner, that teaches the alphabet but doesn't offer macaroni sculpture (or the like). Does the school use the city, take kids on trips, or use the skills of parents (either by inviting them to teach or by encouraging them to bring the kids to their places of work)?

Listen to the teachers. Are they articulate, enthusiastic, intelligent?

Look at the decor. Is the place cheerful? Are the walls covered with diverse and original children's work or do all the hangings look remarkably similar? The latter could mean that the kids are copying the teacher rather than creating their own art. Of course, until you are actually a nursery-school parent, fingerpaintings will tend to look alike but if you look closely, you'll spot individuality and variety. Look at the cubbies, the posters, and the messages on the wall, too,—you'll learn a lot about the school.

Finally, sit in with your child one day, and answer a simple question: Is he bored?

# HOW TO GET YOUR CHILD INTO A NURSERY SCHOOL

When you begin to research nursery schools, you may at first be intimidated by the "acceptance process." Will your child be rejected by the school of your choice? And will she be permanently damaged by the rejection?

No one knows for sure about any child's reaction, but we do know that what's important is how a parent handles and conveys that rejection to her child. Obviously you don't want to convey a sense of failure and disappointment to a three-year-old. It is vital to keep in mind that perfectly wonderful children can be rejected by perfectly mediocre schools. It's essential to believe in your kid—and his or her possibilities and potential—no matter what.

However, noble parental virtues aside, there are definite tricks to getting into the school of your choice. Here are some:

- The best way to get into a good nursery school is to pick one you know you'll get into or one that takes everybody. There still are such schools, many of them excellent, and your child will meet a variety of city children there.
- The second best way to get into a good nursery school is to have a child who is bright, outgoing, and charismatic, with the personality of, say, a Kennedy. Otherwise, no kid is a sure thing.
- From our interviews with directors, it is clear that class and status are factors in whom they accept. It is rare that a child whose grandfather delivers the weather

on network television is turned down. It is even rarer to witness the rejection of a toddler named Rockefeller. One director said many parents use middle maiden names or family names on the admittance application. A good middle *nom de nursaire* to write on your application, would be, for example, Vanderbilt.

- Each director really has a different selection standard. One charismatic, grandmotherly director we interviewed had a preference for kids who needed her and the school. She was drawn to toddlers who would benefit from the environment. (She also admitted that the right bank account helped since the nursery was in a synagogue that was seeking wealthy benefactors). Another director we interviewed was looking for bright kids; another was looking for a more integrated class. Look at the kids already admitted or talk to the mothers of those kids. They may give you some clues about the director's personal prejudices and preferences and how to cater to them.

Luckily, at three, your child can only be herself; she can't fake status and will be admitted someplace where she'll belong. And if, months later, St. James of Kensington belatedly calls about a vacancy and your toddler is now happily ensconced at the West Fourth Street Nursery and Mother's Hangout, most mothers and experts recommend that you leave her where she is. There are enough changes and goodbyes in city life as it is.

The three goals of a nursery school are important, but they should, we believe, be considered within the context of the individual and uneven growth of any child. Don't become obsessed with whether your child has mastered the separation-from-parent process, whether he has enough friends, or whether he's been exposed to every possible form of age-appropriate knowledge in nursery school. Remember these are lifelong goals—and they can take any of us a lifetime to master. Frankly, we've yet to meet anyone who has completely separated from both of his parents, mastered every social situation, or learned everything he's supposed to know.

If there's one thing a preschooler has, it's time. And the same with a preschool parent—time to offer your kid many, many more opportunities. And time for you, too, to grab your opportunities.

## WHAT NURSERY SCHOOLS REQUIRE FROM YOU

Another major consideration is what *you* get from your child's school. Different types of nursery schools afford different levels of parental involvement. The most time consuming (and, some say, most rewarding), type is the cooperative nursery. Shirley Wright, director of the West Village Nursery School in New York City, a cooperative founded in the 1960s, highly recommends it: "There are many working parents who choose cooperative nurseries purposely and put in their two mornings a month (the father one morning, the mother the other) as a way to be with their kid during the day," she says. "It not only lets you see the effect of other kids on your kids; it lets your child see that you want to be there, that both his parents are working to make his world better, and that he's part of a whole community." Cooperative nursery schools are also emotionally involving. You are involved in the decision-making process, involved with other parents, and sometimes involved with the politics of the school.

Other, noncooperative types of schools may encourage you to participate in one of three ways: they may urge you to attend certain parent/child events, such as fathers' brunches or family Thanksgivings; they may ask you to volunteer once a month in a class (without being responsible, as in a cooperative, for curriculum, teacher hiring, and so on); or they may be primarily interested in having you contribute to PTA-type activities—meetings, manning a booth at a Saturday fair, donating money or objects, et cetera. If you're a working parent, the first two kinds of participation will affect you the most; and if your school's director tends to be a little judgmental and pushy about them, that's a sign of a good school, one that has your child's interests at heart. The more advocates your child has—whether or not you can accommodate them or agree with them—the better for your child.

Many nursery schools also hold parenting workshops. You might want to attend one to see if it's well run, if parents are showing up, and how meaningful the topics are. If any workshops are held during the day, are housekeepers allowed or encouraged to attend? They should be.

One special note about housekeepers: If your housekeeper is dropping off or picking up your child every day, she is part of your involvement with the school. You need to talk to her about the information you want to glean from the school every day—about how your child's doing. And you need to talk to the school's teacher and director about your housekeeper. Many teachers have told us that they hesitate to express their opinions about housekeepers unless they are specifically asked. "I feel funny," said one teacher, "telling a parent that their housekeeper seems incompetent or that she discourages a child from playdates with certain other kids because, say, she doesn't speak the same language as that other kid's house-keeper, or whatever. I know I should speak up, but I also know parents are doing the best they can to keep good house-keepers; they're defensive already—and, well, I'm afraid my own prejudice, that housekeepers aren't as good as mothers, will come out." On the other hand, your housekeeper may feel excluded by the school. It's best to get prejudices or feelings out in the open. Teachers aren't always right—or negative—and they may have important information.

Once you've gotten your child safely ensconced in a school he likes, with a level of involvement that makes you feel comfortable, just relax and stop worrying. If you feel basically happy with your choices so far, you're doing fine.

After all, soon you'll have to face the real pressure: first grade.

# SMALL APARTMENTS, BIG MESSES

*I* hate going to sleep at night and hearing my mother washing the dishes; the kitchen's right next to my bedroom, and it sounds like the water's running right over my pillow. That's my only gripe about growing up in an apartment.

—Edith W., New York City

*M*y friend gave my son a thirty-five-piece airport set for his second birthday. I could have killed her. Look, I want him to develop his fine motor skills, too, but why can't he do it with five pieces? Does he really need thirty-five pieces in a one-bedroom apartment? Do you know what it's like to step on a little helicopter blade in the middle of the night?

—Vikki J., Chicago

*W*hen we first moved into our two-bedroom apartment from a studio, we were thrilled with our feeling of expansiveness. I would stand in the kitchen and Mark would go into one of the bedrooms. "Mark!" I'd call. "Where are you?" Hearing him answer from more than three feet away was exciting beyond belief.

—Genny Y., San Francisco

*M*y biggest problem living in an apartment with kids was that whenever I yelled at my kids or my husband, I didn't want the neighbors to hear. I became very good at hissing.
—Denise L., New York City

Most often, it's after their second child that parents acutely feel the effects of living in a city apartment. That fourth body, that fourth personality, can strain the fabric of a family. As one New York father said, "I don't care how big your place is, if there are two kids squabbling, any apartment is too small." If you live in a small apartment in the first place, so much the worse.

But some parents feel another kind of pressure after their second child: "It's like sitting in a life raft with the maximum number of people," one mother told us. "You know that one more body will sink it." It's hard to believe that you may be basing your decisions about how many children you're going to have on the size of your apartment.

"For me, it's just another practical consideration," another New York mother said. "A medium-size apartment is all we can afford, all we'll probably ever be able to afford. Maybe if we had more money I would have considered having more children, but I feel a commitment to raise my kids in the city. My circumstances here dictate that I can only do well by two kids. I've made a thoughtful decision based on what's best for me and my kids."

"We'd never leave because of a space problem only," a teacher and father of two told us. "If we left the city it would be because of a combination of things. Like two private school tuitions, a rent hike, *and* a small apartment. I could see myself thinking, 'What am I struggling for?' if the tradeoffs became too great."

When you have a family, dealing with the problems that are endemic to apartment dwellers can be intense. But there are solutions—some practical, some attitudinal. Both can work.

## BABYSPACE

You just have no idea how much space a new baby can take up until you have one and acquire the accoutrements of infancy. How much you acquire for your baby depends a lot on your style. You might be inclined to buy everything you see, if this is your first child. There is a moment—not at all unpleasant—when every new parent discovers he or she has suddenly vastly broadened interests as a consumer. Besides the novelty of it all, everything you can buy is so—you know—*cute*. You may also find yourself feeling oddly competitive about such things as baby appliances: If your friends' two-month-old has a baby swing, doesn't your own child deserve one, too? Beware of these feelings. Your baby does need a place to sleep, a place to be bathed, an infant seat to be fed and carried in, and a stroller. Beyond that, you can either fill up your apartment or not. Your house will inevitably look like a day-care center anyway, or worse, especially if you have more than one child, but you can easily get away with the basics.

## WHAT YOU CAN DO WITHOUT

*A CHANGING TABLE.* You can make a changing table out of any torso-high table, desk, or bureau. Stretch a bedpad over it for your baby's comfort. If you're not exceptionally tall, you can comfortably change your baby in her crib. You can buy a plastic mat to slip under her; it comes in a plastic case so it's handy and portable.

*A HIGH CHAIR.* You can feed your child in his carry-cradle seat till he's old enough to sit up. By then he'll be ready for a sassy-seat—the plastic seat that hooks under a table or countertop.

*A BABY SWING.* "I can't even remember how many times I tripped and fell over the aluminum legs of Jared's swing," one mother told us. "We got one because I was tired of holding him all the time and someone told me he'd be happy to sit in a swing for hours. Some babies are, but Jared wasn't. The swing's inconvenience definitely outweighed its effectiveness. I'd borrow one for a few days before I invested in one."

## SAFETY FIRST

*"What do I like about living in a small apartment with a one- and a two-year-old? My place is completely babyproofed—for my kids, anyway—so they can go anywhere and I have my peace of mind."*

—Cathy N., New York City

The best thing about having a baby or a toddler in a small apartment is that it's relatively easy to make your place safe for your child. Childproofing a place never seems to occur to parents until their baby is nearly mobile; things are going along peacefully and then, *wham!* Suddenly your entire house is a minefield. There are peculiarities about your place you never noticed before: Wall sockets every two feet; doors without latches; rooms crawling with wires; the cabinet door under the sink where you keep the Clorox flying open *Exorcist*-style whenever the baby staggers by; tables with razor-sharp corners exactly at the baby's eye level.

You can take one of two attitudes about this. You can either turn your house into a maximum-security prison—putting up gates or locking the doors to every room, taping down all lamp wires, storing away anything smaller than a VW, removing the knobs on your stove; or you can do the minimum of babyproofing and then teach your child what he may touch and what is off limits. There are advantages to both choices. The main advantage to the first is that you and your child will be able to enjoy relative freedom in your home. You will be able to sit in one room while your child is in another and be able to think about something other than which long wooden object you could use to pull her away from the wall if she's stuck her tongue in a socket. Your child, too, will enjoy privacy sometimes, and will need it. One mother told us that she once found her very active two-year-old sitting alone and quietly singing to himself: "I'm alone, all alone, and my mom's in the other room."

The advantage of teaching your child at a very early age what's acceptable to touch and what is off limits is that you are less inconvenienced—that is, you're not always tripping over or opening and shutting gates, and you can leave your stereo equipment in a place where you can actually use it.

But there's a minimum of critically important things to do to babyproof your house, no matter how big or small it is. (Of course, the smaller your apartment, the less work you'll have to do.)

1. Put safety plugs in all unused wall and counter sockets.
2. If possible, move wires out of your baby's reach—not only because she may bite into them but also because she could pull down a lamp or a piece of equipment.
3. Lock all cabinets the baby can open. This goes even for cabinets where you store safe things, such as canned food. If you don't lock these cabinets, when your child is about eight months old, you'll constantly be picking up stuff from the floor after your kid takes out and rolls over to someplace where you'll trip on it and hurt yourself. But don't lock away the pots and pans. Babies can spend hours (over the course of time) playing peacefully with pots that aren't hard for you to put away.
4. Keep medicines and poisons in a locked cabinet, preferably high off the floor.

5. Install child guards on all windows; or open windows only from the top, locking the lower windows.
6. If you're lucky enough to have stairs, install gates at both top and bottom.
7. If you live in an old apartment building and have any question about whether the paint on your walls or windowsills is lead based, call your city's health department.

There is a special city problem relating to windows: Around ten months, as soon as your child can stand by himself and is beginning to cruise, you will begin to notice, first, that some of his smaller toys are missing. Then, if you are one of the less fortunate, other items such as one of your shoes, your wallet, or anything you own that is small, portable, and close to the floor will disappear, too. They've disappeared because your child has thrown them out the window or into the garbage can. As a new parent, it might never occur to you that your child would throw things out the window, simply because you would never do it. But, as an experienced city parent already knows, your kid will do a lot of things you would never think of doing.

## AS YOUR CHILD GROWS

There are three main things you have to consider if you live in an apartment with kids: comfort, privacy, and as one mother of a teenager put it, what you do with the possessions of a lifetime.

The problem isn't that you sit around dreaming about what it would be like to live in a ten-room apartment; the problem is that one day you'll step barefoot on a jack or twist your ankle on a piece of Lego; or you'll open a drawer looking for the bus map and find yourself standing in the same spot a half hour later, gripping rusty washers in one sweaty hand and a year's worth of Baggie ties in the other. That's when living in a small space feels unbearable: In a single act, you find yourself in conflict with your surroundings. When this happens, it's a great temptation to take out the way you feel on the person who left the jack on the floor or who empties his pockets every evening into the junk drawer. If you don't put effort into making your place comfortable for you and your family and continue to work to maintain your comfort, apartment living is going to get you down and out of the city. Maintaining a city apartment is like dieting: It works best when you follow the rules every day, which is impossible. So if you slip and stuff yourself or your closets with junk, be patient. Remember these three things which we've adapted from *Getting Organized* by Stephanie Winston (New York: Warner Books, 1978):

- Avoid the psychology of disorder. If you are very strict and authoritative with your kids about things being organized and neat, they may develop a lasting feeling of negativity about it. They may use messiness as a way to rebel against you, and neatness could become one of your battlegrounds. In a small place, this can be murder.
- Make it more difficult to put things where they don't belong than where they do belong. This is a lot easier than it seems.
- Think of how each area of your apartment functions and whether it serves its purpose. In her book, Winston suggests you think of each room separately and consider clearing the room, taking everything out except the furniture, then deciding what you want in the room and what you don't; redistribute the latter to wherever it belongs

(toys to the kids' room, books to the living room). Put things that you want in the room near objects you use them with. Once the room's uncluttered, think about what kinds of activities go on there (the things you've redistributed will be a clue) and decide whether you want them to continue in that room. Sometimes you can relocate activities simply by moving the thing that draws the activity—such as the television—to another room.

## THE KID'S ROOM

Even at a very young age, your child deserves respect and privacy when he wants it and when it is appropriate. If his room is a place where he has no control or privacy—that is, if he has no say about where things go or if the room is not child-proofed or messproofed enough to let him be disorganized or messy without causing permanent damage—then it's worth taking a look at whether your influence is interfering with your child's freedom to enjoy himself at home. It's hard, especially in a small place, to allow for another person's aesthetic, and especially a three- or four-year-old's. But when you look in your child's room, if you see evidence of his play—of his enjoyment and his growth—and you can allow yourself to appreciate that, you'll be less inclined to want him to have a designer or picture-book bedroom, anyway. A kid's room should look as if a kid lives in it.

We're going to assume that you don't really care whether or not your child's toys are organized; you just want them out of the middle of the room. It's important, when your child is old enough to help clean up, that his room be organized so that he can do that. If you run a low shelf around the room, he will be able to put his own toys away. He should be able to open and close his drawers. Hooks should be at his level. Feeling competent about such a small thing as hanging up his jacket will increase your child's self-esteem.

In *How to Organize Your Kid's Room* (New York: Ballantine, 1985) Susan Isaacs gives suggestions about good ways to help your young child learn to clean up:

- You can label hooks and drawers with pictures cut from magazines or with photos of objects. Hang a picture of a hat over the hat hook, and a sweater on the sweater drawer.
- Talk about what you're doing when you're putting things away: "We put the cars in the plastic bin, and the dolls in the basket..." Verbalizing, Isaacs says, helps children understand the process of cleaning up.
- Make cleaning up, whenever possible, a time of fun and shared activity. It works better with a two-year-old to say, "I bet you can't put all those little men in the bucket," than to say, "Let's put away your toys." (By the age of sixteen simple commands work best, advises a mother of two teenage sons.)
- Keep crafts materials such as Play-doh and paints out of your child's reach until he understands the limits about where he can use them—or else allow your child his special space where he can use them freely.

To accommodate your child's need for change as he grows and the freedom to make a mess of things, you can use these strategies:

- Use map hooks on a map rack or bulletin board and use mounting clay instead of nails for hanging pictures.
- Use what Susan Isaacs calls the "exchange system." Store

toys your child doesn't often play with on a high shelf; bring them down every three months and put others away instead. The toys you bring down will seem fresher to your child. (On the other hand, several parents reported that the toys they put away they found three years later during a massive house cleaning. Rather than enjoy their "new" toys, their kids had outgrown them. One father who tried to keep his son's toys to a minimum told us, "I'd put a toy away, right. Then the next rainy day we'd be cooped up in the apartment and I'd be thinking, 'Is it three months yet? It *feels* like three months.' The system doesn't work for a desperate man.")

- Use plastic bins or baskets you can move around rather than a stationary shelf. You can use a stack of bins to make a room divider, a headboard for a bed, or a private cubby for your child in the corner of another room.
- Cover a wall with vinyl tiles so that your child can draw on it and wipe it clean.
- Buy a rubber mat you can throw down anywhere so your child can play with paints or Play-doh without you worrying that he's going to destroy the floor or the rug.
- Stretch cheap canvas across two standing stretchers for a movable room divider.
- Put in ladders or steps wherever you can—up to the child's bed or to a platform area. If you have a child over the age of one, you already know: Kids love ladders.
- Raise the child's bed to counter height. It will be easier for an older child or adult to make, and you can store clothes or toys underneath it.

One of the things that makes it most difficult to organize an older child's room is that the child's needs are constantly changing, and in small ways and big ways he will often be altering his environment. One city mother said of her teenage son, "He doesn't need to take drugs. He lives in a mood-altering room." You may be satisfied just to keep the door to your kid's room closed all the time, but if you're not, you may want to reorganize the room to make it more livable. Isaacs maintains that it's crucial to remember that the room should be manageable for your child—he will learn to feel competent by finding the things he wants and by being able to return them to their places. So, she suggests that you consider your child's skills, his active interests and his waning ones, his personality characteristics, his schedule, his social patterns, and his habits and priorities. Look at his room and figure out which activities take place in which part of the room, whether or not each part of the room is suited for what goes on there. In this way, you should be able to figure out why there are always papers all over her bed (she doesn't like to work at her desk because it's away from the window) or she leaves her makeup on the bathroom sink (there's no mirror with good lighting in her room). Talk to your child about your observations and about how she feels her room could be made more comfortable for her.

## PRIVACY FOR YOUR CHILD

As your child grows, he will increasingly use his room as a haven, a private place to be and to keep his things. Having space of his own is a crucial part of his development into a separate, independent person. Establishing a spot in your house that is your child's alone helps establish the child's identity, says Dr. Elaine Heffner.

If your child has to share a room with a brother or a sister, you can help him have some private space by either making or buying a tent to put over his bed. You can set up a small tent for him in a corner of your biggest room or else establish a corner of a room that is your child's by blocking it off with a room divider. Keep out of that space unless you have your child's cooperation or permission.

If you have no extra space to give your child, you can establish what Heffner calls "symbolic privacy" by giving your child a cabinet, a drawer, or a cubby of her own. If you're lucky enough to have family within commuting distance, you can also establish (with your relative's permission) a room that is your child's when she is there.

## PRIVACY FOR YOU

There seems to be two schools of thought among city parents about privacy. For some parents, privacy is no problem; they simply lay down the law about their accessibility and follow through. In general, these parents:

- Establish rules about privacy when their kids are very young, and don't break the rules except in an emergency. They say that, by the time their kids are nine or ten, their behavior about privacy has become a habit.
- Respect their child's privacy as much as their own. One mother told us she never enters her child's room without knocking first, so it doesn't seem unreasonable to her daughter that she should do that before entering her parents' room.
- Stick to a schedule of "private times," which they and their children spend in separate rooms. A mother of two-year-old twins told us: "We live in a small two-bedroom apartment. I've had to establish certain rules about privacy and quiet. Whether they're tired or not, I make my kids stay in their room for forty-five minutes every day. Maybe they only nap 50 percent of the time, but we all need the time away from each other."

- Install locks on doors and use them. "I hate locking our bedroom door," said one mother. "It's like I *feel* for two people, me and my kid. It brings up all the feelings of rejection I had as a kid when I wasn't allowed in my parents' room. The part that feels for me really needs some privacy and intimacy with my husband. So I tell myself that we all have to learn how to cope with rejection and we all have to learn how to make time for ourselves. I feel ambivalent about it, yes. But I lock the door."
- Go out whenever possible. "When I need to be alone," one mother of a teenager told us, "I take a walk around the block. If I lived in the suburb where I grew up, I could never do that. Everyone would be looking out the window saying, 'Why's she walking around the block by herself? How come she's not home giving her kid dinner?' I would just feel conspicuous. But here in the city I go out and I'm free to be anonymous if I want to be. I guess I've traded being able to hide in the attic or wherever for being able to hide on the street. I enjoy it. The street's so much more interesting."

But for other city parents, privacy is a difficult issue. It's more likely to be an issue if you live in a place that necessitates you use all available space for the whole family, so that even your bedroom is not inviolate; or if your apartment is laid out in such a way that you have to walk through one room to get to another; or if you're just too casual or too rushed to be knocking on a door every time you want to enter a room—or if you, like many *single* parents, especially, feel inordinately responsible for your child's happiness. You cannot seem to find a half hour to be alone, to cook a meal without interruptions, to take a breather in the bedroom. A mother who admits to having a separation problem with her daughter told us: "I was forced to cut a deal with her. That's what finally worked. After eight o'clock, she had no access to me except in an emergency. She didn't have to go to sleep and she could listen if she wanted to to see what I was up to, but she'd be breaking the contract if she tried to engage me in conversation or activity. I was the one who needed support to keep the deal going; I needed to feel that I deserved the time alone."

If privacy is a problem, keeping toys out of your bedroom may also demand drastic measures. "In our apartment," another mother told us, "the coziest room is our bedroom. We are always having to shepherd the kids out. And I simply do not allow toys in our room. If I see one, I get it out, right away, like it's a roach or something. It's the one room where I don't let any of the kids' things accumulate."

## STORAGE

*"A lot of what we own is hanging from the walls. The rest is under the bed. It's a big bed. Built up very high."*
                                    —*Michelle T., New York City*

What do city parents do with the things and the clothes we don't happen to be using at the moment, with the toys and the equipment and paper and the projects our kids have made, the things it's more economical to save or it would break our hearts to throw away?

While it would make sense for city dwellers to be the kind of people who love to edit their possessions, instead most of the people we talked to admitted to having a packrat mentality. One mother said, "For a long time I would save a couple of chairs that needed to be recaned or I'd find a great old table out on the street and I'd take it home and I'd be thinking, 'This'll be great when we get a country house...or when we get a bigger place.' I'm not exaggerating—our place started to look like a junk store, between what I brought home and what my husband did. When our daughter was born, we had an apartment sale. With the money we made we bought a crib and a stroller. We're much more selective about what we save now."

---

### SPACE INCREASERS

- Many parents store out-of-season clothes and extra furniture with friends or family out of town.
- One mother of three-year-old twins stores all the clothes and blankets she has no immediate use for at the dry cleaner. "Forget to pick the stuff up?" she says. "Are you kidding? We'd have nothing to wear!" She's also lucky enough to have a small balcony off her living room. "It's our apartment's saving grace," she says. "We use it as a shed. And when my husband builds shelves—which he seems to be doing every weekend—that's also where he works."
- Depending on what kind of building you're in, you may also be able to store things in the basement. "Once or twice a year I wonder, 'Is my butcher block still down there? Is my bike okay?' and I have to run down to look. The little bit of anguish is worth it to me," says one crowded city parent.
- When you live in a city apartment and you can't afford a country house, the only way to get some space may be to go home to mother. It can actually seem pretty nice, when you know you live somewhere else. "Almost every summer weekend, my wife and daughter and I go back to the suburb where my wife and I

---

met in high school. We hated it when we grew up there, but after living in the city for fifteen years, we feel different about it. Our daughter calls it 'the country' because there are lawns and trees. Seeing it through her eyes has made it a much more pleasant place for us."

- When you've used up every bit of space in your apartment and you feel trapped, one of the best things you can do is to buy a car. Even if you never use it to get out of town, you can always store things in it. Most families with cars do both.

Everyone says this, but it's true: If you want to take advantage of the city, you have to trade things off. One of the things you trade off is space. One city mother said, "I actually like the limitations of a small apartment. I feel the opportunities outside our door are limitless. That's why I live in the city. It comforts me to come home to a place where I am absolutely sure of all of the boundaries. In a way, I guess I want to live in a place I feel confined in."

Other parents also marvel at how they've grown used to small spaces. "The first year I lived in my large Upper West Side apartment, I spent many an afternoon wandering from room to room, sitting for a while in each one, just because it was there," said one.

Or, as another woman said, "When my husband and I moved from a small studio into the loft we'd been saving for, we found we were always getting into arguments about not being able to hear one another or misunderstanding one another. 'You're going deaf!' I'd tell him. 'You're mumbling again!' he'd say to me. We finally figured out that we had to speak louder to be heard in a larger space."

And just as you adjust, your child will, too. "Your child might be the type of person who needs a lot of space to run around in and feel free in," says Dr. Elaine Heffner. "Because you live in a small apartment doesn't necessarily mean that he can't have the space he needs. You must be more resourceful about taking him to places he can run in: parks, museums, a gym class, swimming. Once you recognize the need, it's not that difficult to do something about it."

A city father adds, "I love it when one of our friends has a baby. It means we get rid of another box full of junk."

Although we talked to a lot of happy and optimistic people, no one found it easy living in an apartment with kids. Once or twice a year, maybe on the first bitter cold night of winter, when your apartment happens to be clean and you've just made a pot of soup and your kids are playing happily—in a neighbor's place down the hall—you can sit in your favorite spot and look around and take a deep breath and think, "It ain't much but it's mine. At least until the lease runs out."

# CITY KIDS AT HOME: UNBEATABLE INDOOR GAMES AND ACTIVITIES

*T*he hardest thing for me as a city mother was filling up a day spent indoors. Not just my kids' and their friends' day! Mine. They'd play in three of our four rooms, and I'd sit in the kitchen waiting for my son's play date to go home! It was the only room that you couldn't hear the noise.

—Joanna L., mother of two boys

*T*he best game indoors is sardine tag. One person hides and the rest of us are it. We have to find the person, we separate, and when one of us finds him she gets into the same hiding place until all of us are in the same place except for the last person left. And then that kid gets to be the first person to hide the next time. Parents love hiding games I know because there's lots of quiet times in them, even though there are also lots of kids. They also like you to ask which closet you should absolutely stay out of. That's probably a smart idea.

—Sarah G., San Francisco, age fourteen

*L*et your kids play by themselves. Parents worry about quality time together. I just like it when I play and my mom or dad is around. That's quality time for me.

—Steven M., Chicago, age sixteen

By the time he is twelve, your city kid will have spent approximately twenty-five-thousand hours playing indoors. And because we often live in small spaces, we can become painfully aware of every hour there. If we live on the upper floors of apartment buildings, we find our older kids—eight to twelve-year-olds—less likely to flit from indoors to outdoors and back again the way suburban and country kids do. When they're out, they stay out (we hope), and when they're in, they seem to be in for the duration. This is especially true if you live in a city neighborhood where young kids are reluctant to hang out alone.

So your kids are in. And while they're in, we know it's important that they relax, play, and feel the homeyness which they can only feel when they're securely in the family nest— whether they are playing by themselves, with friends, or with you. City kids especially, say many experienced parents, therapists, and teachers we spoke to, need that time at home because they are so stimulated by the city's events, by the street life, by after-school activities, and by all kinds of cultural activities. And yet indoor play can seem constricting for parents and kids both. In small apartments, we often must limit kid space or we'll feel that they're invading ours. Living with apartment neighbors, we sometimes feel sensitive about even reasonable play noises. As one mother of a four-year-old said, "One of the first things Marcel learned to do while he was playing in our apartment was to put his index finger to his mouth and whisper 'Tiptoe. Right mommy?'" Finally, kids playing in small spaces seem to make larger messes faster.

All those factors explain why many of us have often settled for the peace and calm of having our kids watch the tube. We may even have uttered in a desperate moment (not us, not us) "Bored? Haven't you checked the *TV Guide?*"

There are some mothers who never stoop to TV—but very few. There are other mothers who love the loud sounds of ten kids romping in a small apartment—also very few, but they make great friends. Most of us enjoy having kids indoors in small bunches (having our own friends around helps a lot) at

103

reasonable decibel levels. As a result, we're always searching for ways to make a day indoors work—for ways to maximize fun and family togetherness with a minimum of tension.

What follows, with thanks, is the collective wisdom of city parents who have very ingeniously created strategies for the indoor day—from fashioning "indoor/outdoor" space to dealing with noise to designing fabulous games and activities especially suited to city kids and their families.

## SPACE

Joanna F. lived in a very small apartment and was going bonkers with her five- and eight-year-old sons. "We just didn't have enough space, even though we'd designed every inch of it with them in mind. Then one morning, while I was doing the laundry in the basement, I noticed several doors. It turned out they lead to large empty rooms. One of them was rented by the family in the penthouse; the husband used it as a wood-working room. I decided to make a friend for my children. And, sure enough, the gentleman, a man in his fifties, invited Ben and Matt down and helped them build a toy sailboat together. Then I thought a little more. What about all those other rooms? I found the largest one, spoke to several parents, and we rented it. It was incredibly cheap. The kids and parents decorated it. It was big enough for a Ping-Pong table, a dart board, and jacks on the floor. We put up two schedules: one of when parents could supervise and one when the Ping-Pong table could come down so the girls could play indoor hop-scotch. We called it 'the mother's office.' It was fun—and it established a family of families in our building."

So the first answer to lack of city space may be to make sure that you know how much space you really have. Explore your building. Talk to your super. Even check out your roof. How much would it cost to build a fenced-in playground on your roof? Private schools do it. Why not apartment houses? Naturally you'd need to look into security and insurance concerns, as well. There is another "outdoors" that comes with any apartment, and that's the hallway on your floor. Many city parents depend on hall play. A youngster can slink his Slinky down the back stairs (there's nothing better for a Slinky than an apartment house's back stairs, but make sure your child is old enough to be near stairs!) play hall hit-the-penny and ball-rolling games, or just plain fantasize. A hall can be your back-yard, and with the right neighbors, your kids can even decorate it.

## NOISE

No matter where you live, there is the law of childhood: Kids will fill with noise any space you give them. You can suggest quiet games (discussed in the next section), but realistically, whatever the restrictions, sometimes they'll need to move and run and play or they'll get to you another way—by being antsy and fussy, for example. One trick is to schedule that noise—and then hire a babysitter so you don't have to endure it. Just because you're not working, just because you have no plans, doesn't mean you can't be good to yourself and leave for a while, donating that time to your child's freedom. Let a fourteen-year-old handle it—a teenager whose ears don't feel attacked by the thumps and pounding of eight-year-olds. You'll not only be doing a service to yourself and to your child, but to that teenager's mother.

What about your neighbors, you say? Learning to be considerate of neighbors is important, both for kids and for us. But that doesn't mean always *ssshing* your children. You have to have faith in what you consider "reasonable noise" and the rules you've established to maintain that. Otherwise, you'll turn into a hair-pulling mother who wails, "Don't run, don't bang, don't breathe." It won't work. If you have a sensitive neighbor, keep him informed. Tell him when a couple of children are coming by for a date, for example. Tell him about an upcoming party. One mother whose four kids have four large birthday parties a year sends her formerly furious downstairs neighbor free tickets to a city event whenever she knows a kid's party is coming up—and an invitation to drop by for birthday cake afterward. Even if they don't use the tickets, they appreciate the gesture. Another mother has her kids send funny thank-you notes and homemade Christmas gifts to an upstairs neighbor who endures their birthday parties. It's amazing how much less noisy your kids seem when your neighbor knows them, likes them, and understands they're trying their best.

## GREAT GAMES

Still, there are many hours indoors. Fortunately, there are many reasonably quiet and entertaining ways to fill them. The city kids and parents we've interviewed are amazingly inventive, adapting games to their particular living situation with creativity and finesse. We found loads of active, indoor games and activities that city kids can play, taking up as much room as you want to allow them and requiring a range of parental participation. Some mothers keep a list on hand of five or ten games, and when they hear the inevitable "I'm bored" or the click of the TV set being turned on, they check the list for alternatives. Here are some that struck us as the most fun and the most original.

## ACTIVE SPORTS

Even indoors, kids need action. When they're little, they can run around the house in fantasy play. But as they grow older, almost any outdoor sport can become a workable, fun, and not destructive indoor game, especially with the help of a Nerf basketball, football, or baseball. Here are a few inventive options:

*INDOOR MINIATURE GOLF.* We mean miniature here—there's no way to turn your house into a driving range and not have regrets. Start by getting your kids a small putter and a rubber ball. Then build indoor golf obstacles like the following:

1. Bend a piece of cardboard almost in half. Take the shorter half, bend it again, and cut a hole. Put a cup under the hole, stand up the little "hill," like a triangle, at the end of any hall and let your kids putt down the hall, up the hill, and down into the hole.
2. Take a wide piece of balsa wood and lean it up against a sand bucket. Place this in a hard-to-reach corner, and try to hit a ball up the wood and into the bucket.
3. Use containers—anything from a grocery delivery box with two sides eliminated to an empty soup can with top and bottom removed—as obstacles. Try to putt the ball through the object.
4. If you've got sectional couches, separate them and leave a narrow space for the ball to be hit through. Otherwise, create a little tunnel with two chairs.

Once you start this game, your kids will come up with many more ideas. You can play together, and they can keep score. It's fun, relatively quiet, and it can take hours of constructive construction beforehand as well. Store your golf course as you build it and keep adding as ideas occur.

*INDOOR BASKETBALL.* A ten-year-old who likes sports will create a basketball court anywhere: He'll shape wire into a hoop and hang it in the bathroom over the faucets; he'll abscond with your abandoned rattan planter and attach it to his loft bed; he'll buy a kids' hoop and climb a stepladder to paste it over the hall door. If he hasn't thought of all this already, help him. Indoor basketball is fun, and it's also relatively quiet with a Nerf ball. If the moving feet start driving you nuts, set basketball hours.

*INDOOR FRISBEE.* There is a Nerf Frisbee game with a large felt board. Kids tend to discard the board and just have Frisbee catches. Diving for a Frisbee is noisy—there is no getting around it. We suggest hall Frisbee between three and five o'clock in the afternoon, when most neighbors are away. Otherwise, try double-bed Frisbee: You can't get off the beds to catch the Frisbee.

*DART BASEBALL.* Since darts in small areas are dangerous, use a felt board with matching balls. Draw lines out from a center point on a felt circle, then fill in each pie shape with baseball hits and outs: singles, doubles, triples, home runs, fly outs, ground outs, double plays, stolen bases, et cetera. Each kid can play his inning until he's "darted" out.

*BALLOON ANYTHING.* After a birthday party, most parents notice that the leftover balloons are immediately turned into games by their kids. Just keeping one in the air is a good game. So why not keep balloons on hand? Place a piece of furniture in the middle of an open area. A coffee table is a good divide to use as your net, and you're ready for balloon volleyball. Or take your basketball hoop and play with a balloon instead of a Nerf ball.

*TIDDLYWINKS.* This seems like the ideal quiet indoor sport. You can suggest it—the kids might like it for a couple of days.

### INACTIVE SPORTS—FIVE GREAT GAMES TO PLAY AROUND THE TABLE

The following games are fun for kids to play alone or for families to join in together. They can take place around a kitchen table and require only simple tools.

*FUNNY CATEGORIES.* This game is truly ridiculous and gets funnier the cleverer you are—and the lower your taste. In fact, the more tasteless, the better. First, you each draw a large five-by-five grid on your own piece of paper. Across the top, you each write a five-letter word with no duplicate letters (for example, *place* is acceptable, but not *sleet*.) Then, down the left, you write a category next to each row: disgusting habits, ailments, obnoxious noises. You even can add some straight categories, such as perfumes or strange professions. Then you each fill in the grids, writing a word in each row beginning with one of the letters of your five-letter word. For example, if you've written *place* across the top, you need disgusting habits starting with the letters *P, L, A, C,* and *E.* This bawdy and tasteless game has brought many a family happily together.

*SENTENCES.* Pass out a sheet of paper to each parent or child. Each person must write down a man's name. Then she folds over that name so it can't be seen and passes the paper to the left. Now, with your neighbor's folded sheet in front of you—without looking at the name—you write down a woman's name. Pass it again to the left, and add the word *were* to the sheet in front of you. Fold it over and pass it on again. Next add an action verb and the word *at* to the sheet you get and pass it on as usual. Finally, add a place and the word *because* to the sheet you've passed and send it on in turn. When each of you receives the finished sentence, you read it aloud. A popular game! It beats those ad-lib printed games by a mile and is not as complicated (though sometimes as threatening) as adult versions of this game, which require writing a sentence at each pass.

*BRILLIANT SOLUTIONS.* This is another version of the game above. Have each child or parent quietly write down a serious problem someone might have, such as, "You're being chased by an elephant"; "An evil curse has been put on you by a witch"; "Your teacher is coming to tell your parents that you haven't done homework in a month"; "Your dog has an upset stomach"; and so on. The requirements are simply to use the second person, *you.* Then give each person another piece of paper and let him or her write one sentence that would be a brilliant solution to the problem. Now pass each problem paper to the left and each solution to the right. And then have each child read the two papers he's got. Naturally, the wrong solution to the wrong problem will read rather hysterically. (For example, your teacher is coming. Give her paregoric every four hours.)

For boys under ten, many of these games do tend to turn a little raunchy. They love it.

*TAPE-RECORDER GAMES.* These are basically improvisation games and will be as much fun as you make them. They succeed best if there's a ham in your family, and the tape recorder seems to heighten the "hamminess." Here are two versions:

*Detective:* Have someone play a detective investigating a murder, interviewing everyone at the table with the tape recorder. That's it. Don't organize it. Don't explain it. It just plays out. It's up to the detective to make up the murder. Three kids can say they did it, if they like. It doesn't make sense—it has no ending—but it's still fun, and kids adjust to the discrepancies. The less you know, the better.

*Saturday Night Live* versus *General Hospital:* Kids age eleven and older love to imitate current TV shows. It's fun to do a cross between two of them, with one kid who loves playing the crazy comedian playing opposite another kid who is a soap opera character—sex idol, murderer, or financial scoundrel.

*INVENT YOUR OWN BOARD GAMES.* You can take any board game and copy it over, with changes appropriate for you. For example, one family rewrote Clue. They named the suspects after people they knew and changed the murder weapons to things like a wet noodle and poison ice cream. Monopoly is plenty of fun just as it is, but you can change the streets to stores in your neighborhood.

## SEMIACTIVE SPORTS

There are other games, of course, that take up little space or actually define the space that kids can use and are big favorites in apartments. These include such standards as Ha-ha, Telephone, and the game Tent. Most of us have played Tent. We've emptied the linen closet of blankets or a pretty bedspread or two, turned over some chairs, and built a tent the kids can play in. It's the little amenities that make it special, say several mothers: a cozy lamp; some dried flowers; tea sandwiches; et cetera. Tents are great fun to play in, and great fun when they collapse, as they inevitably do.

## OTHER INDOOR ACTIVITIES
## (CRAFTS, HOBBIES, AND SKILLS)

City parents, we found, have a special approach to some other indoor activities. Some activities work better indoors than others, whether because of the space, noise, or light considerations or because of city kid preferences. City kids do seem to have their own taste. The following activities seem to be universally recommended:

### Hobbies and Crafts

Give a child a hobby or a skill and he is *not* yours forever—which is, of course, your ultimate goal. Starting at seven or eight, when kids begin to develop the desire to collect things or to practice a skill for longer periods of time, they can develop passions and strong interests. Parents are blessed when their son or daughter becomes obsessed with something, whether its baseball cards or cartooning. Helping your kid develop a passion for something—indoors or out—is a great gift you can give her or him. Indoors, particularly, it can fill hours and hours of time in a pleasurable and memorable way.

*Collections.* Kids can enjoy collecting anything, especially in the city. One young woman remembers visiting the Cloisters in New York at age seven, the time when young collectors seem to emerge from their cocoons. She fell in love with the unicorns depicted in the tapestries. She and her mom came home and started a unicorn collection. Another recently grown-up city kid remembers collecting erasers. It turns out that there are thousands of types of erasers, and hundreds of stationery and toy stores to go searching for them. Another boy, unusual as it sounds, began collecting knives after he'd been mugged—not kitchen knives but rare and beautiful samurai swords and turn-of-the-century cowboy knives. Trust us—the kid is a very healthy and together teenager today, and that collection got him over a rough period.

There are the standard collectables—baseball cards, dolls, stamps, coins, beer cans, bottle caps, and rocks. The advantage of these collections is that there are often clubs, conventions, and magazines that kids can get involved with. But in a city there are also many unconventional items to collect, especially if you and your children are city explorers. What's wonderful about such collecting is that it fills both indoor time and outdoor time—building something to store the collection in, reorganizing the collection over and over again, cataloguing it, fantasizing about it, as well as shopping and combing the city's neighborhoods. A collection can not only keep a child occupied and involved for a long time but it can extend a child's attention span and her ability to go deeper and deeper into a subject; if it's a unique collection (and any collection in its way, is), it can also foster a sense of individuality, of personal passion, that you'll hope your child will always have—which may be one reason you've chosen the city life in the first place.

Some collecting tips: If your son or daughter expresses a fledgling interest, *always* start slow and small. One father warned, "When my girls were small, I was so eager to bring them up in a nonsexist way that when they showed the slightest interest in a sport or craft, I'd go to the toy store. I remember my five-year-old daughter liking the baseball cards a friend of mine's son had. That Christmas I bought her a box of them and a mint set of the year's players. It sat there. I tried to get her interested again, but she never was." Said the daughter, "He turned it into this colossal interest I had to have, and I guess I didn't see it as mine after that." Be in touch with how great your child's readiness and interest really are. (Make sure

113

the interest is his or hers, as well as yours—a mistake most of us have made at least once.) Often when you ask your child what to buy for his collection, the answer will reveal a lot. If he is really involved with something, he won't ask for the biggest or the most expensive item. He'll ask for what he's ready for, what he needs.

## Arts and Crafts

Many apartment dwellers find their kids learning crafts outside the home, at after-school programs, museums, and so on. Pottery and woodworking take up room after the toddler stage. Here are three simple, space-expanding arts ideas from city mothers:

1. Hang large sheets of paper from the wall, either rolls of photographer's background paper or ten-foot sheets of wrapping paper, and let the kids draw. This is fun at a party, but it's also fun on an ordinary Tuesday.
2. Donate a wall to your children. Some parents find this idea too permissive but it can be a big hit with kids. Give your child a wall in his room or in the adjacent hall that he can take Magic Marker to, that his babysitter (the one who draws so well) can add to, that his friends can sketch on. Having his own wall can be a special treat for your child especially if there are no other kids he knows with the same privilege. It is likely to produce *You are so lucky!* from other kids, which might tend to make you very proud of yourself.
3. Play Squiggles. This is a simple drawing game that kids and even teenagers love. An adult draws a bunch of squiggles on a piece of paper; then the child has to draw

something using the squiggles as part of the sketch. The more complicated the squiggles, the better.

## Cooking and Baking

Practically every city parent recommends cooking and baking. There's always some kitchen task to be done, whether it's peeling a carrot or pouring the cup of cold water into the Jello. It only takes a mother who's willing to spend twice the time preparing something than she would normally—and one who has a good sense of humor about sugar and salt on the floor.

Kid cooking should start off with the simplest recipes. Even twelve-year-olds get bored with complicated concoctions. What seems to work well is a simple idea slowly and creatively added on to over the years. For example, one youngster specialized in salads. He started off decorating them, and now he's making them—from Waldorf to chicken to Caesar. When one young son of friends of ours was only four years old, he got up especially early to make eggs for the family. He made a perfect omelet, except for one thing—he forgot to put butter in the pan. It was burned but it tasted of effort, creativity, and love. They ate it of course, and liked it. Since then, omelets have become his thing, his area of cooking expertise.

What's great about specialties such as omelets are that they're basically simple, but a child can continue to get better at them, becoming creative and inventive on his own. Other specialty possibilities include crêpes, soups, and anything with spaghetti sauce on top. In fact, homemade spaghetti sauce is a great and simple specialty for any kid and is more valuable than chicken soup in a house with children. The great thing about this last indoor game is that it can surely turn into dinner on a semiregular basis.

• • •

Whatever the indoor activity—whether it's a modified sport, an organized or improvised game, a craft, or a skill—it may very well be an important memory for your children, perhaps the most important. One youngster we spoke to said, "Some kids will remember going to the theater and stuff after they grow up. But my happiest days were when me and my friends built a tent in our living room and my mom would be in the kitchen and we just played for hours. It was home, and that's gotta be the best part of being a kid."

# CHAPTER 7

# HAPPIEST BIRTHDAYS

*I* grew up in Park Slope, a little city in Brooklyn, New York, and I still miss the parties I had, the friends I knew, even at eight. Every year, as an adult your circle narrows—but as kids, in the city, we had the world in our house on our birthday.

—Susan G., New York City, now age twenty-five

*D*on't invite too many kids. Parents who invite the whole class—to be nice—are ruining their kid's party. You don't really care about all those kids and they don't care about you. They forget about you at your own birthday. It's better to just invite five friends.

—Herbie N., Boston, age twelve

*M*ost parents think that kids are too busy to eat the cake. This is not true. They don't eat the cake because it's an ice cream cake. The ice cream in it is icy cold and horrible. Kids hate ice cream cakes. Trust me—it's true.

—Paul H., New York City, age fourteen

*I*'ll be honest with you. I can't remember a party I had. And I had a very happy childhood. Are they important?

—David K., Chicago, age fifteen

City birthdays can be magical. If you've been raised in a city or visited one on a birthday, you may remember a special walk through a lit-up theatre district at night, the thrill of a special show or a musical, dining out at a "sophisticated" restaurant. As a kid you knew that cities were the place grown-ups took you to have a special time, the place grown-ups went when they stayed up late. As a city parent, it's still a mall of celebratory events, both day and night—and a reminder of why we're lucky to be raising our kids here.

Even throwing parties in the city can be special—not only because of the variety of entertainment around but because, as one city mother said, "At my daughter's parties, the kids were all so different: different styles; different ethnic, racial, and religious backgrounds. Their parents were rock musicians or lawyers or mailmen. As hard as birthday parties sometimes are, they were wonderful. They were like bringing the best qualities of the city indoors."

There are two ways to celebrate birthdays in the city: throwing a party for kids and spending a night on the town with the family. Many parents do both. As for the first option, parties, may we just start with a cautionary note: Parties can be fun, or anxiety producing or both, but we notice that they have become a fad of late. Parents seem compelled to give a party *every* year. Just remember—there are many ways to celebrate in a city, and if you prefer not to give a party every year, don't! And one more note of caution: City birthdays can lead to social pressure, since there are so many choices that you or your child may feel the need to keep up with the Jonahs in his class. ("Jonah rented the *Queen Elizabeth*. What are you going to do for my birthday, Mommy?") Just keep in mind that a good time and a celebration of your child's birth and existence is your only goal, and that kids can have a good time in a million simple ways.

## PARTIES

Before you plan a successful party, you first need to think about the following three basics:

1. *Who is your kid?* Throw the party that will work for her. Says San Francisco child psychiatrist Patricia Heldman, "Remember to separate yourself from your child. What

119

your memories of birthdays are, what you feel the pressure to have, is different from what's best for your child. *Ask your child what she wants.* Think about whether [she likes] to be the center of attention." Limit the size to what she can handle. Involve her. Trust her. Let her help plan, decorate, make invitations, and so on. And, especially, let her pick the guest list. If your kid doesn't want someone at the party, respect that. Don't be a "nice" mother and invite the kid nobody likes. It's your kid's birthday party—not Brotherhood Day.

2. *Who are your child's friends?* If you don't know them, speak to other parents or to your child's teacher. She'll know their favorite films and movie stars, or what games they love this week. If your son's entire class has been playing Stratego all month, you might want to have it available at the party.

3. *Know your limits.* Know what you are willing and able to handle in a relaxed manner, because the way you feel and the way your child feels you're handling the party is as important as the flavor of the cake or the kind of entertainment. The older your child gets, the more he wants to be proud of you; and he cares most about whether you get along with his friends, whether you're a screamer or "don't touch my furniture-er," or even someone who can't leave the kids alone. As one young boy said, "The trouble with Jonathan's mother was she was always there. Just as we would start to play something in his room, she'd come in again and say, 'How's it going? You boys want another cupcake?'"

In other words, before you plan, figure out how you, your child, and his friends can best relax and enjoy themselves. Parties do come with some anxiety. Says Dr.

Heldman, "But if you know yourself, and how you feel about birthdays, your own and your child's, it makes it easier. And keep in mind that a birthday party is just one event in a whole history of showing love to your children; and if you throw a party in accordance with your parental values, not social pressures, the chances for feeling that the party is a success are greater."

### THE PLAN

Keeping these three factors in mind, you can then begin to tackle the second key element in a successful party: your plan. Even in limited space, all it takes are three basics to planning any good birthday party. You need:

> **a theme,**
> **one main event,**
> ***and* one clutch event.**

For example, if the theme for your eight-year-old is magic, your main event might be a magician or a movie such as *The Great Houdini*. Your "clutch" event (that special finale that kids love) could be how you distribute the kids' prizes: hiding them around the room, asking the magician to make each kid's prize appear out of a hat as part of the show, having kids go fishing for prizes, and so on. In the sections that follow, we'll suggest "clutch" events for parties with various themes.

Generally speaking, if you have a theme, one main event, and a clutch prize event, you can't miss. In small city spaces, simple and surprising is always best. Even a movie and three kinds of flavored popcorn as your clutch event will do it.

The city has everything you need for parties, from the most lavish to the simplest. For example, if you collect the calendars of your city's major entertainment areas and educational facilities—zoos, parks, museums, puppet theaters, nature centers—there's bound to be a child's event on the weekend of your child's birthday. (Many are not listed in the weekend newspaper.) You might also want to check out some unusual locations for city kid entertainment. International organizations such the Japan Society in New York City, for example, might be having an origami event or know an origami artist. One New York mother was watching a local kids' show and saw a wonderful "noise" artist—a man who imitated the sounds of trucks and elephants and car crashes—and found him in the telephone directory.

## MAKING A SCHEDULE

Once you've got your theme, your main event, and your clutch event, you might want to write up a schedule, just in case. On it, list the main event, minor busy events (playing pin the tail on the donkey, making party hats, et cetera), and clutch events so you know that the kids aren't sitting around for the last two hours of a two-and-a-half-hour party. The schedule might be simply:

Noon: The kids arrive;

12:15: They eat lunch;

12:30: They sing "Happy Birthday" and your child opens his presents;

1:00: They have their "main event" (a movie, entertainment, or even games)

1:45: They have second and third events (unless the movie is still going!) such as balloon games, arts and crafts, and pin the tail on the donkey. If these fail,

2:30 (or about thirty minutes before the party ends): You stage the clutch prize event;
3:00, Finally distribute goodie bags. As the kids leave, read a story for the kids still waiting for their moms.

Although out-of-the-house parties are fun (and often necessary if your home is small), house parties, if done with a little imagination, seem to be the ones kids remember most, whether in the city or country. Use your Yellow Pages. You'll be amazed at what you find in any large city—a juggler's supply house that gives lessons or demonstrations of new products, a store that sells prizes or closeouts for seventy-nine cents, a wholesaler who sells plastic jewelry by the half case (which makes great prizes for eight-year-old girls); a street vendor or a caterer who'll rent you a cart and sell hotdogs or pretzels and egg creams.

Remember that any party, no matter how simple, can be fun, with just one good idea and one clutch event. And when you plan, remember your kids' dignity. Ideas that suggest you start a party with all the kids coming in the door and crawling under the birthday boy's uncle are generally embarrassing to any kid.

Here are some classic parties, themes, and clutch events that the city moms and dads we spoke to most heartily recommended*:

*Two great books for theme ideas are *Birthdays*, by Marilyn Atyeo and Anna Uhde (Atlanta, Ga.: Humanics Limited, 1984) and Susan Smith's and Melinda King's *Happy Birthday* (Oswego, Ore.: White Pine Press, 1983.) The ideas in these books tend to be a little cute, but pick and choose what suits your style. Another good source of party ideas that are down to earth and written as first-person experiences by average parents is *Kids Day In and Day Out*, ed. Elizabeth L. Scharlatt (New York: Simon & Schuster, 1979).

## PRESCHOOLERS' PARTIES

- Try a *FARMS AND ANIMALS* theme, even in the city—at this age, animals are a natural interest. Sing "Old MacDonald," "The Farmer in the Dell," "Bingo," or "The Farmer Takes a Wife."

  Some successful clutch events include planting seeds in little flowerpots and letting the kids take them home; finding a kid in your building who's into shadows and having her make animal shadows on the wall as the kids identify them or make the corresponding animal noises.

- Try a party based around *FIRE ENGINES, CARS,* and *TRUCKS.* Rent a fireman's costume or just wear the big red fireman's hat and be the host of the party. For a clutch event, have the kids make fireman's hats (these can look like any other hat but should be red). Or fingerpaint with vanilla pudding that you've added red food coloring to. Play hide and seek, but call it "rescue" by firemen.

- Some other themes for little kids include teddy bears, dinosaurs, letters and words (put simple words they know on the wall and play charades, in which they have to act out the word) and storytelling.

- General tips: Always have balloons around, both for improvising games and for decorations. You can often find a stationery store that will print each kid's name on a balloon.

  Make sure you discuss with the birthday child which of his toys are off limits to friends during the party. Hide them. Make sure you also provide the birthday child with her own loot bag.

  Generally, party experts suggest that the number of children invited equal the birthday boy or girl's age.

## PARTIES FOR FIVE- AND SIX-YEAR-OLDS

When your child reaches five, you're ready for some more imaginative themes and clutch events.

Five- and six-year-olds love puppet shows, dress-up and make-up parties, clowns, balloon artists, folksingers, et cetera. But we spoke to several mothers who used the city in special ways. One New York City child, for example, wanted to be a taxi dispatcher when he grew up. For his birthday, his mom called a friend who was a taxi driver. The party started with four boys taking a taxi ride, listening to the mysterious voice of the taxi dispatcher coming over the loudspeaker. He detailed, with imaginative taxi jargon, the streets and obstacles they would pass on their way to the site of the party, the apartment of the birthday boy's grandmother, and even let the little boy speak into the microphone.

Another young boy loved trucks and had a very unusual birthday party at a local truck stop at his city's farmer's market. The kids had their birthday cake while they looked out the window of the diner, surrounded by the biggest collection of car carriers and tow trucks they'd ever seen. They then took a tour of the trucks, birthday hats on, and met some friendly drivers who let them sit in their trucks.

At this age, there are many great clutch events. Here are some that many city mothers recommended—and that can work until the birthday boy or girl is ten or eleven:

- Fish for prizes. Two grown-ups hold up a big sheet decorated with fish (or with images of whatever the party theme is). Behind the sheet are prizes. Each child has a turn using a fishing pole that has a loop at the end of the string. The

125

child tosses it over the sheet, and a third parent attaches a prize to it.

- Play What's in the Box? Kids from five to twelve love this game, even though there is only one winner. Buy a prize or game. Wrap it in paper. Put it in a bigger box. Wrap that box. Put that in a bigger box, and so on. Now you have a multiwrapped prize. Let the kids pass the box around, each kid unwrapping one layer. The one who unwraps the last layer wins the prize. Great game.

Although some experts say prize winning is upsetting to some kids, we don't find that to be true in these cases because the events are so much fun. Still, you can keep that sensitivity in mind by awarding other prizes for anything, such as being the best sport, the fastest player, the first to arrive, the last to leave, so that everyone gets something. But do make sure your loot bag is uniform for all. Kids don't mind one kid winning one special thing, but they feel cheated when they don't get equal treatment when prizes are *supposed* to be equal.

And here are some nonprize clutch events for five- and six-year-olds:

- Have the kids bring costumes. At the end of the party, the kids all go into one room (usually the bathroom), get dressed in their costume (leotards are enough, usually), and plan a show for the hostess. Five girls in leotards in a bathroom inevitably will produce giggling hysteria. If you knock very quickly and say, "What's going on in there?" the giggling will never stop. At this stage, when they come out to put on a show, only they will understand its theme, story, and plot. But they'll have fun.
- Build a house. If you are at all architectural, bring in a bunch of packing cartons of all sizes and shapes to use in

your construction. You can cut out windows and skylights and put in seats. You can even serve lunch inside.

## PARTIES FOR OLDER KIDS

### Seven-Year-Olds

Seven is the year you can start to gear your party to your child's hobbies or career aspirations: ballet, sports, or magic. You might also have a balloon artist, rent a movie, or cook a meal. Generally, it's still easier to keep the party small and at home.

Possible clutch events include fishing for prizes, putting on a show, or decorating a wall. (Cover the wall with huge sheets of paper from a photo supply house. They come in all kinds of fabulous colors.) Also try the games listed in our indoor games section of Chapter 6, Detective and Squiggles.

At seven, complicated interpersonal politics and sensitivities start to become most apparent at parties. Include everyone in group games and activities. Try team games, such as charades or a pentathalon racing event consisting of games such as hot potato, passing a matchbox from nose to nose and blowing a piece of cotton from the first member of a team down the line to the last.

### Eight-Year-Olds

At this age, great themes are building a model; gymnastics; origami; or a visit to an old ship, train, or plane museum.

One of the most enjoyable parties for an eight-year-old we heard of was called a "rehearsal" party. Invite your child's friends over for rehearsals of a play or a TV show. Provide some costumes, give them some possible ideas, and let them rehearse a play that they will perform for their parents when they come to pick them up! One idea: A play called *The Problem at the Palace*. It is the princess's birthday, but nothing will please her. The king and queen keep bringing in entertainment and gifts, even a clown,—but she scoffs at it all. Every kid gets a chance to act, sing, or dance her heart out to please the stubborn lady, but the birthday girl grimaces after each one until, finally, the whole group performs something together—which makes her smile at last. For the finale, pick a show stopper that they can all sing. A sentimental one works best, such as, "When You're Smiling, the Whole World Smiles with You." This play never fails. Even the parents like it.

### Nine- to Eleven-Year-Olds

A popular theme for this age is home Bingo. But lots of parents start taking their kids out in the city. They recommended going to shows, participating in or watching a sporting event (baseball, basketball, bowling, wrestling, and karate matches are all fun). Read your city paper's sports pages, because you're likely to find ideas for unusual events to attend.

One mother called the public relations department of her child's favorite ball team and, even though it was off season, asked if they gave tours of the stadium. They did. It was an unforgettable day for her son—and since they allowed only three kids, an easy day for that mom. If you're not up to the tour, you can still call the public relations department of your child's favorite team (or ballet group, or band, or whatever). They'll send autographed pictures, which are great prizes for any sports-oriented party.

If you're holding the party at home, many parents urge you to take the crew outside for a while if weather permits. Two St. Louis city parents half finished a snow fort in the nearby park before their party started. During the party, they took the kids out, finished the fort, and served their ice cream and cake inside.

In the spring, try any of the following: a treasure hunt in the backyard or on the street, a pony ride, or a hansom cab ride. One of the best outdoor surprises we heard of was a trip to a park hill, where the parents laid out ten huge plastic garbage bags. They poured water down them, making them fabulously slippery, and the kids had the biggest waterslide ride they'd ever had—right in the middle of the city.

## Ten-Year-Olds

Going to shows, plays, and sporting events still works at this age. For a home party, this is the age to take out the costumes again, even with boys. One woman we spoke to described her son's most memorable party: She invited four ten-year-old boys for a sleepover—and let them get at a bunch of female costumes. Ten-year-old boys dressed as girls are hysterical. They can imitate the opposite sex all too well.

Another popular theme for age tens is a treasure or scavenger hunt. Invite four or five kids. Give each of them a sheet with instructions reading, for example: "Start at the couch." There they might find a clue under the cushion, such as, "Your prize starts with the same letter as the object it's hidden behind." Have them proceed until they discover their prizes.

Two great clutch events for this age group are funny categories, and Detective, both described in the indoor-games section of Chapter 6.

## Eleven- to Thirteen-Year-Olds

Many of the home and away parties mentioned above still work for this age group, but the kids can be much more on their own, and they prefer it. Or you can hire a caricaturist, a sleight-of-hand magician who does only coin or card tricks (this magic still works with older kids, as it does, of course, with adults), a disk jockey, or a psychic.

If you're not morally opposed to gambling, you might also consider poker for the twelve- to thirteen-year-old crowd, or a gambling night. Set up three tables—one for poker, one for blackjack, and one for roulette. That's a great sleepover party for boys. You can supply the chips and give prizes to the winners.

## OTHER IDEAS TO MAKE THINGS EASIER

Over and over again, the city moms we spoke to emphasized the following ways to make your job easier:

1. Get help. Hire a teenager, the birthday child's older sibling, or a babysitter; enlist your mother, your mother-in-law, your father, your father-in-law.
2. Don't be afraid to serve lunch. It kills time, and kids love it. Just have it early, before the kids start to run free, or you'll wind up with toddlers trampling frankfurters. And be sure to serve simple food. The classics work best: cocktail franks, pizza, hamburgers, fried chicken.
3. Forget the birthday cake. You probably will have to provide one at a couple of parties to believe this for yourself, but the fact is, they can cost a fortune and the kids don't eat them. One successful party-giving mother suggested that you put a candle on something else—regular ice cream or one of the presents. It's cheaper, more surprising, and fun.
4. Keep the party going by breaking it up with different events, moving to different rooms, and so on. And keep it short.

## SOME SPECIAL CITY CONCERNS

Let your neighbors know you're having a party and World War III hasn't started. Invite them in if you'd like, or if you know it will be noisy, give them fair warning to go out (or, as we suggested in Chapter 6, buy them tickets to a concert).

If you want to play in front of an apartment building, let those neighbors know too or tell your building superintendent.

If your apartment is small, check out other space in the building. There is nothing like a home party. Is there a friend who will rent or let you use her apartment for two hours? Can you barter with her for something special, such as a weekend's worth of dinners?

At away parties, have the kids dropped off at the party location and picked up at your house at the end of the party (if that's where you plan to wind up). Home is an easier place to wait for moms.

If you have no choice, and you must shlep ten kids to a magic show, make it as easy as possible: Use cabs or get someone whom you *don't need* at the party to drive the whole group to your destination. That way, there's no waiting for your mate to park the car before he can join you at the party. (That way, you can avoid a disgruntled, "Did I miss the party? Tsk, tsk, tsk. That's a shame. Did it go okay?")

## OTHER CITY BIRTHDAY EVENTS

There are so many ways to have a city birthday. Have a family celebration at a special restaurant; buy an extra present, stay up all night before the birthday to look at the stars; invite one or two kids over for a sleepover, or take a kids' twosome to a hit play. Plan a couple of events or treats, but make the last one a surprise. And remember, especially if you work, if you're divorced, or if you just generally feel you aren't doing enough for your city kid, don't overdo the birthday party and presents. This day is an expression of your love, not of your guilt. And there are many, many ways to say "You're special" on a birthday.

# CHAPTER 8

# STREET LIFE

*W*hy do children so frequently find that roaming the lively city sidewalks is more interesting than backyards or playgrounds? Because the sidewalks *are* more interesting. It is just as sensible to ask: Why do adults find lively streets more interesting than playgrounds?

—Jane Jacobs[*]

*Jane Jacobs, *The Death and Life of American Cities* (New York: Random House, 1961), 85.

*P*eople are always saying to my father, "How can you raise David in New York City? It's such a jungle." Sure, it is a jungle. Monkeys raise baby monkeys in a jungle, and if you asked a mother monkey, she wouldn't say, "I think I'll move to the suburbs when I have children!" What's wrong with a jungle? It has everything and everyone in it. And our parents raised us so we can handle it. I agree with the monkeys—I'd rather grow up in the wild than someplace safe with only a bunch of other monkeys that look like me.

—David K., New York City, age sixteen

*I* was buying groceries for my mom in the Korean store, and this guy and woman came in and pointed this little gun at my ribs. They said, "We won't hurt you. We just want the guy's money. Go in the back of the store and look like nothing's happening." So I went to the back of the store and started picking broccoli. I had broccoli in both hands, under my arms, under my neck. I just kept picking and not looking until the guy who owned the store ran out and screamed, "We've been robbed." Sure, it was horrible. It wasn't funny. But it was funny anyway. And I'd never seen a gun before.

Sue, Cambridge, Massachusetts, age sixteen

## KIDS ALONE

City streets—they're what makes a city kid. When the streets are safe, full, alive, lively, and exciting, we've shared them with our children, happily and proudly. And when they're dark, quiet, unpopulated, and our kids have to tread them alone, we've sometimes dreaded them.

Jake, as a young boy, hung out on his block; played dodge ball and box ball; learned juggling from a street juggler; sold lemonade on Broadway from his own little stand; roamed street fairs; saw people, people, and more people. As a teenager, he explores various New York City neighborhoods with a sense of freedom and adventure. At times, when he and his mother walked together, she says she had the sense that she was giving him a tremendous gift—a neighborhood—a colorful, heterogeneous, unruly neighborhood that was contributing in a wonderful way to his character and that would someday enrich his memories.

On the other hand, one day, going shopping by himself, Jake was mugged at knifepoint. That was the only time his mother ever really thought, "What am I doing to my child by raising him in New York City?" That night and whenever she worried about his safety from then on, it was very hard to remember the good things about city family life.

If the word of the 1980s is tradeoff, then city streets are the tradeoff of city parents. For all their energy, activity, variety, and mix of cultures, there's also concern about what your kids are confronting every day. They have to negotiate traffic in a city where drivers sometimes don't care about rushing a red light. They may pass prostitutes or pornography; they see crazy people, poor people, homeless people. They may be mugged. The very "real" life that may have drawn us here seems too much, sometimes, to impose on a child.

Said one mother, "I look at our kids, all grown up, and I like them. They're accepting and open and interesting; they were stimulated not by conformity but by eccentricity and excellence and a million potential role models. But I know they also paid a price—they couldn't just run out and play and wander. Has it made them more fearful adults? Life isn't simple, and I don't know specifically what caused any adult hangups they have today. But I do know that though I still wonder sometimes if I did right by them, they feel lucky to be raised here."

Tradeoffs—sophistication versus danger; a variety of things to see and experience versus less freedom of movement. Is it worth it? For some parents, the key to survival with those tradeoffs is beating the ambivalence. Said one father, "If you're going to be conflicted for twenty years, it'll make it harder. It's important to keep things in perspective, make your decision on where to live, and minimize the negatives. Two of my four kids were mugged; so they learned quickly to spot trouble and to avoid it. Most kids learn how to do that. And for that sacrifice, the plus is they grow up in a great city. All of them are now adults who would never live in any other kind of environment."

She's right. He's right. Their kids are grown and safe. But we, the mothers of young and growing children, worry. Will our kids be safe? Are they okay *today?* What are they seeing *right now* and how do they feel about it? A lot of us parents who grew up in the suburbs, who are first-generation city parents, feel sad that they can't blithely ride their bicycles or walk down any street they want the way we remember doing where we grew up, in smaller towns, in innocent times.

At those times, when we romanticize our childhoods or worry that our kids are missing something, it helps to remember two things: that we had fears then, too, of passing a certain park or wood at night, of a local bully or a gang, of walking into an empty house, of the strange man who offered us candy—even of monsters and dragons and dinosaurs. *All* kids have fears. They are sometimes imaginary, sometimes real, but they are universal and parents everywhere have to deal with them. It also helps to remember, for those of us who chose to live our adult lives in cities and leave our childhood homes, that it's because of those childhoods that we've picked a more urban environment, that we're happier here, and that as happier people we make better parents.

Still, we need to know how to handle these real concerns and fears about city life. We *want* to educate and to toughen our kids, but often our instinct is to protect them fiercely. We know that we shouldn't overprotect them so they have room to become street smart and thus enjoy the city's riches with a sense of competence. But, sometimes, as one parent put it, "you'd rather have an incompetent, overprotected kid than a hurt one."

Besides learning how to make our kids street smart, it does help to come to terms with and be honest about the negatives of the city—to talk about it, deal with it, and get past it so we can really enjoy an urban life. And we know it's not easy to do. Here's some help, we hope, in how to do it.

### DEALING WITH THE BAD STUFF

In large cities, even on a simple trip to school, a city kid can encounter more different scenarios, more of the range of human behavior, than another child will see in a year. Should we be concerned about this? Does this diminish or deprive a

137

child of innocence? Says Dr. Ralph Lopez, a physician and specialist in adolescence, "Teaching kids how to handle themselves on the street, and put what they see in perspective, is important. It's teaching them independence and survival skills. Is it too hard for a kid to comprehend that there are some crazy people around? Of course not! Does seeing these things make them too adult or sophisticated? No! My daughter knew which streets she could walk down, and who might be dangerous or weird, but she also knew those were rare extremes. And she was also still a child. Innocent like any other child. She played with dolls, fantasized, et cetera. In Wyoming, they teach young children to shoot animals. Is that too adult or sophisticated? Becoming street smart is not having to be too adult— it's just being realistic. And becoming adaptable. In fact, that's one of a city kid's greatest assets."

### ENCOURAGING INDEPENDENCE

To enjoy the streets, we need to encourage our kids to feel independent and capable of handling themselves. Around the ages of six to twelve, they need to start to separate from us. At the same time, we want them to be safe. Advises Dr. David Kelley, a child psychologist in New York, "Suburban kids are driven everywhere. If you're concerned about your kids' safety—and, just as important, if your kid is worried—then there's nothing wrong with chauffeuring city kids around. *It's most important to build a 'fence' of safety around your child so that he can go through each normal stage of development with a sense of security.* When you have doubts, take your kids to their destination. They can play independently, without you, when they get there."

## TEACHING STREET SMARTS

At the same time that we maintain that "fence," we can also slowly start to build street smarts. Perhaps the best book on this subject, Grace Hechinger's *How to Raise a Street Smart Child* (New York: Facts on File Publications, 1984) should be must reading for concerned big-city parents. It deals with the harsher facts of city life—how to avoid being mugged; how to deal with a mugging when it occurs; how to ride the subways and the buses; what kinds of self-defense are practical for kids to learn; and how to convey all that information in a positive way, so a child is mastering skills, not submitting to fear and insecurity. Many other books, especially the ones written for kids at the height of the safety panic, seem less helpful. We gave several city youngsters these books. Even though several of them had been mugged, they all felt the advice was extreme: "Never talk to strangers"; "stay two armslengths away from anyone you don't know," and so on. All this struck them as unnecessarily rude, scarier than it need be, and impossible to do. Said one kid, "We just won't do it, we don't want to do it, and honestly, we don't need to do that. You have to trust us a little. We've been walking these streets our whole life."

## SOME BASIC APPROACHES

From early childhood we can begin to set up some specific house rules—rules that will vary, depending on your child and on where you live ("You can cross West 82nd Street when the light is green, but not Broadway by yourself until you're bigger. You can ride your bike, but only on the park side of the street.") Then, at each stage, we can help our children to increase their sense of independence. ("Now that you're seven, you can cross Broadway." "Now that you're eight, you can walk the dog in front of the house.") The rules we set depend on each child as well. Said one parent of two very different kids, "To Jason, a shy, cautious, sensitive soul, I was always saying, 'Walk, Jason. You'll be all right.' And to his sister Jennifer, who was fearless, I would say, 'You're not taking your bike to school this year. Period!'"

Every kid and every parent is different.

We can get to know each particular child's concerns by playing out some scenarios. Sheryll Kraizer, author of *The Safe Child* (New York: Dell, 1983), calls these "what if?" games. Before you're about to go shopping, you might ask your five-year-old, "What if we are separated at the store, what should you do?" Or, at home, "If mommy's asleep and the doorbell rings, what should you do?" Ask your kids to come up with "what ifs?" of their own, too. Listen, come up with solutions that you think are reasonable, and listen some more. You'll hear your children's fears and can talk about them together.

Some lessons every generation passes on: Teach your children their address and phone number; teach them not to run out into the street; never go with strangers; not to walk down dark or abandoned streets without an adult present; and never to flash money, expensive radios, and the like on the streets.

## WALKING TO SCHOOL

The first real independent act for city kids often comes when they express a desire to go to school by themselves. This seems to be an exciting time for them, but one that makes us parents nervous. The process of teaching them their school route helps us as much as it helps them. Here's a composite of how many parents handled this rite of city passage:

1. Generally, kids ask to walk or to ride alone to school at around eight years of age. If you think they're ready, then on the next few trips to school together, start to point out landmarks—either stores or people they see regularly en route. As you walk, ask questions: "What's the name of the street we just walked down?" "What's the most recognizable store?" and so on.

2. Tell them very simply and matter-of-factly that, if some adult bothers them, not to hesitate about saying, "Leave me alone." And if the person doesn't listen—to shout it. If they're too shy to do that, tell them to walk immediately into one of those landmark stores you've found together. City kids, say most parents we've spoken to, tend not to obey adult strangers automatically. Our kids are questioners, and this is the perfect time to encourage that trait.

3. Before they go off on their own, introduce them to a few of the owners of stores they'll pass—either those you know personally and have patronized or those who seem friendly.

4. Map out the safest route for them to walk alone. This is not always the shortest route. Then walk it together.

5. Have them take you to school one day, without your saying anything about where to turn or where to get off the bus. If they can do that:

6. Then let them go off by themselves.

Chances are, no matter how well you've prepared, you'll still be a little nervous. Feel free to follow them—at a distance, of course. Half the parents we spoke to tailed their children to school the first time or two they walked alone. In fact, one mother who got caught said, "I felt like Spenser for hire. I thought I did it rather well until we got to school, and he waved good-bye to me." Said her now-grown son, "Knowing she followed me came in handy. For months afterward, whenever anyone looked scary, I'd wave to an imaginary mother and mutter, 'Bye, see you later, Mom.' I figured, nobody's gonna hurt me with my mother half a block away." City kids come up with their own ways, realistic or imaginative, of handling their fears and maintaining their egos.

It helps to keep that in mind once they're out there on their own. But if you still feel a little panicky, a little crazy—if, after a few months, you're still tempted to phone the mothers of twelve of his friends when he's a half hour late—keep in mind one piece of strategy recommended by experienced parents: You can indulge your own fears, but *don't* impose them on your kid in an unhealthy way. Make some rules for your child and for yourself. Tell your child, for example, to call or to have a parent call if she's going to be late for *any* reason. When she forgets for the second time or third time, talk about it, but consider imposing some sort of penalty. Kids can handle it and need to know you're concerned. They can even handle reasonable anger expressed appropriately. What they don't need is panic.

One mother recalls, "I was raised by a mother who was afraid of everything—water, heights, traffic, lightning. A low-flying plane could shake her up. And because I inherited some of that, I'm very conscious of not imposing that junk on my son. I really try to calm down when I feel hysteria or my own fears starting to build. I talk to myself. When my son said casually the other day, 'You know, I forgot to get off the bus this morning and wound up in the middle of the park,' I didn't scream, 'My God, the park! You know what can happen in the park?' I thought first; I said to myself, 'What would *Leave It to*

*Beaver's* mom do in this situation?' Then I listened to the outcome of his misadventure, to his feelings, and I left the room. Later, at dinner, I brought it up again. I acknowledged that it upset me and said, 'You know, since you tend to be a little absentminded on the bus sometimes, and that concerns me, maybe we should get you to go to school with your friend Michael but come home alone (since Michael stayed for an afterschool program). What do you think?' He loved the idea. I think we both felt better after that talk.''

## CHOOSING TO WALK TOGETHER

Every once in a while, your kids might still want you to accompany them to school. Walking your children to school, like reading them bedtime stories even after they can read alone, is reassuring and a wonderful way to be together if you can manage it. Said one mom, "He walked with his friends Monday through Thursday. But every Friday we had a date. Walking is like watching TV for kids. They don't have to look at you, so they can say almost anything. I not only learned who broke my vase and what he really got on his math test, I also learned how he felt about God, Mayor Koch, and birth control. Walking was like a key that started his emotional motor running.''

## HANDLING HOSTILE KIDS AND SELF-DEFENSE

What if your kid is accosted by tougher kids? Said one mother, "My son was on his way home from school with two other eight-year-olds and they were standing on a corner, waiting to be picked up by Astros, a sports club for young boys, and they were threatened by two boys. They got scared and couldn't handle it. It was very upsetting. Afterward, I told my son and his best friend what to do the next time: to go into the corner coffee shop or to stop any other mother taking a kid home and say, 'These kids are bothering me.' I did all those things, I handled it as best I could; but the experience had already happened. The next day I signed him up for karate."

Because middle-class children are often taught not to fight but to walk away, we sometimes are afraid they'll grow up passive. One way to get around that is to sign up your kids for self-defense classes and Japanese martial arts programs. Psychologist David Kelley is an advocate of this approach. "It's important for youngsters to learn to defend themselves," he maintains; and karate, taught primarily as a defensive mechanism, helps kids send off a vibration that they can handle opponents. "Too many middle-class mothers," he says, "take away that aura of toughness from their children by telling them, 'Don't fight,' and, 'Be nice.' That becomes part of the child's conscience, and it isn't helpful. A child needs to feel he *can* fight when he has to, for example, against people his own size. Karate sometimes helps restore that 'I can fight' vibration, and it's important never to lose that."

Still, there's always been lots of mythology about how kids should handle bullies. We all were raised on heroic stories of the timid kid who stood up to the bully — but most of us never could. We avoided the guy. You can teach your children karate, but remember, it's also helpful to allow them to be candid about not being able to handle tough kids. You can lead a kid to self-defense classes — but you can't make him the Karate Kid.

We believe that the ultimate goal of parenting is to raise kids who like and trust themselves; and who know, whatever their inevitable personal struggles, that we're on their side. In the city, handling danger will surely be one of their struggles. Their best self-defense will be their own self-esteem. If they learn to respect themselves even if they have city fears, to trust their instincts, and to use their brains — which are, for most

144

kids most of the time, their best weapons—the struggle will be easier.

---

## HOW TO HANDLE A MUGGING

Most experts, including most police, agree that in the case of a mugging by anyone bigger than your child or by anyone possessing a weapon, he or she should be taught to hand over the money. How do you handle the emotional aftermath of a mugging? Grace Hechinger urges parents to keep in mind not only the insecurity that's going to stay with your child but also the importance of dealing with your child's loss of dignity and, often, the sense of being violated. Don't make your kid feel responsible, even while you teach him to change his patterns. Don't make excuses for the mugger (by explaining, "He's poor") because what is most important is that your child be allowed to get out his anger and to restore his sense of pride in himself.

Most parents we spoke to recommend reporting any incident to the police, so that kids feel less helpless and less passive. And most important, during the whole process, listen! Don't get angrier than your kid, more upset than he, or the opposite—don't minimize his feelings so they'll "go away." Listen and be supportive. Be "kid smart"—alert to what signals your kid is sending out and responding appropriately.

It can take up to a month after a mugging, say experts, for a kid to venture out on the streets again without real fear. During that time, be patient. But if it takes much longer, consider seeing a psychologist.

---

## ESTABLISHING A STREET LIFE ON YOUR BLOCK

At the turn of the century, the streets of our cities were filled with children, as well as adults—teeming with them, in fact. The streets were where kids hung out; that's where they found their friends, that's where they found their protectors. Many of us romanticize those times, rough and poor as kids were then. But it's also true that even though kids in those days were exposed to dangerous traffic, to thieves, to prostitutes, to violence, and to gangs, they felt safer. The main reason for that, believes Jane Jacobs, was the presence of mobs of kids and mobs of adults. She believes that the way to revive that old-fashioned street life is to repopulate the streets, just as we've repopulated many of our neighborhood parks. These days, on park promenades and grassy hills and picnic areas, adults take walks, take business breaks, have lunch, go running; parents and babies sit on benches, kids go biking. The more people, the more life, the more liveliness there is, the more our child's play will be enriched in such an environment.

If you live near a park, then that most likely has become the street life for your kids. But if you don't and if yours is a quiet street, you can try to reestablish, preserve, or enhance the street life of your city kids. There are more ways to do it than you think.

First of all, join or start a block association. Through that association, form a play committee and find out how you can have your street closed off and declared a play street. Depending on the city, such arrangements are made through the mayor's office, the parks department, or the local community board. Call the mayor's office for the information.

Secondly, when the weather is fine, take a friend, a chair if necessary, and your kids downstairs. If you live in an apartment, consult your building superintendent to find ways for your kids to play without disturbing neighbors.

If you have the time and the inclination, organize occasional kid events, not just block parties. These can include planting

Exploring the streets of San Francisco. (PHOTO BY ROY MORSCH)

147

parties; box ball, wall ball, and stoopball contests; a father/son stickball game, or whatever. One mother whose son had been mugged and was afraid to go outside alone got her private school to help. They staged a mural contest on her block, putting up plywood around a building that was being cleaned, and got all the kids to come down and decorate it. Many kids weren't interested in the mural, but the crowds on the street drew them out to play.

Organizing activities like any of the above can be a hassle. Most of us don't have the time to do half the things we want to, and these kinds of activities, admittedly, are not the first items on our agendas. Still, if you do have time to become involved in some group activity for kids, we think there's nothing more important, no more valuable contribution you can make, than to revitalize and to use your street.

## EXPLORING THE CITY STREETS TOGETHER

### A MINI-GUIDE TO SOME SPECIAL CITY OUTINGS

"My fondest memories of my kids' middle years were the Saturdays when we went on adventures," says one mother, "not the obvious ones, like to a museum or the park, but exploring the piers buying nuts and bolts or whatever they're called on Canal Street, visiting a Vietnamese neighborhood in Queens and having lunch there, getting up at six in the morning to go to the produce markets to buy food for our co-op, walking the boardwalk in Brooklyn. It was as much fun for my kids as it was for me—we went as equals. And there was always a charge of the unexpected and the exciting. Kids can make you a tourist in your own town, and that's so great."

Said another mother, "My son and I just got on a different bus every once in a while and got off at the last stop and explored. And he and his father played a game called 'What's around the Corner?' They'd go out together for Saturday lunch, find a nice restaurant, and then say, 'Should we eat here, or should we see what's around the corner?' You got a maximum of three 'What's around the corners?' before you had to decide. That kind of thing can only take place in a big city like San Francisco. Talk about raising kids to know they have options—this is the place!"

Every parent we spoke to had one or two special, simple city activities they loved to do with their kids. Here are some of them, with some extra guidebook-type information to make them, we hope, even richer experiences.

### Construction Watching

In most cities these days, there's plenty of building going on. And kids, especially between the ages of six and twelve, can watch for hours. Read a child's book about skyscrapers by yourself or with your child, and it'll give you a better idea of just what's going on. Otherwise, here's a short and very simplified little summary of some of the wonders you can observe if you know what to look for.* For example, you might want to:

1. Observe the huge steel skeletons as they go up. These true-life erector sets are made up of three things: the vertical steel *columns,* the horizontal *girders* that connect the columns, and the flat *beams* that are fastened to each girder.

*Much of the information produced here was derived from several terrific books for kids, including *A Young Scientist Looks at Skyscrapers* by George Barr (New York: McGraw Hill, 1963); Cass Sandak's *Skyscrapers* (New York: Franklin Watts, 1984); and the superb little book *Up Goes the Skyscraper* (New York: Four Winds, 1986) by Gail Gibbons.

2. Look closely at how the steel pieces are being connected way up on the superstructure. This is dangerous work, no doubt about it. Many of the construction men at this stage are American Indians. They attach a girder, for example, to a column by matching the predrilled bolting holes of the girder exactly to the predrilled holes of the column; a tapered steel pin, called a drift pin, is inserted into the holes and then a temporary bolt is inserted. It's a delicate job, and they don't use any safety belts—the belts they wear are just to hold their tools.

3. Watch the foundation being built. Skyscrapers are planted in such solid foundations, with such strong bedrock support, that tornadoes and hurricanes and even minor earthquakes won't shake them. Bedrock, by the way, is the solid rock that's part of the earth's crust. Two types of foundations you can watch for are *concrete columns*—these are steel bars and concrete set in big rectangular holes, to make a type of foundation called a *pier;* and *concrete piles*—these are like huge, hollow, spiral steel tubes that are drilled into the ground by a *pile driver,* a big hammer driven by steam or air pressure, and then filled with concrete.

4. Keep an eye and ear out for blasting equipment. To reach the bedrock or to break up large boulders, explosives are used. First the workmen drill holes in the rock, then they place the dynamite in the holes. On top of the dynamite they place what are called "blasting caps" or detonators; the hole is filled with clay or earth, the two wires from the blasting caps are attached to a blasting machine farther away, and a mat is put over the hole. Then a current is passed through the wires, and the explosion takes place. Everything is done safely and care-

fully and in small doses, and cars and people are kept at a safe distance. One interesting reason for people being kept away, besides their own safety, is that the detonators can act as radio transmitters and a passing radio can produce voltage, setting off a blast prematurely.

5. Notice the various types of trucks and derricks, and what they do. The steel for these skyscrapers arrives on a very complex and exact schedule, since much of it can't be stored on the site. Look at the long flat trailers that can have as many as fourteen tires.

Then, of course, there are derricks and cranes. They are quite different. A *derrick* has a huge, stationary mast. Its boom lines—ropelike cables with hooks attached—pivot from the central mast and can lift huge girders. *Cranes,* on the other hand, are mounted on trucks, and can move; they have booms, but no vertical mast. It's fun to watch a worker place a *sling* (a tied cable) around a horizontal piece of steel, test it to make sure it's secure (often he'll use two slings on either side of the girder) and then send it up. On the end of the beam is a *tagline* that a worker on the street holds to help guide it up.

6. When you see a concrete truck arrive, stick around. Kids will love it and be perplexed by it. Here are some facts that might interest them: *Concrete is made of cement, sand, gravel, and water, and reinforced concrete* is concrete that's poured into forms that hold round steel bars or heavy wire mesh. It has concrete's ability to withstand pressure, along with steel's strength and resistance.

Once the concrete is poured, it needs to dry slowly over four or five days, or it isn't as strong. So often it's covered with moist canvas, hosed down, and sealed with plastic to keep it from drying too fast. Concrete also shouldn't endure freezing weather—that's why you'll often see huge plastic covers from girder to girder. Inside those plastic baggies is a heater blowing air, keeping the concrete warm.

## Bridge Hikes

There's something about crossing a beautiful city bridge, a sense of what man has built; it's a structure both practical and beautiful, a piece of art connecting the city and its surroundings. Many cities have lots of them, of different types and sizes, and it's fun to walk across a different type of bridge each time.

There are some fine and simple children's books about bridges, including Cass Sandak's informative *Bridges* (New York: Franklin Watts, 1984) from which we gleaned a lot of our information. Although you never want to overwhelm kids with facts, if they ask or if you're curious yourself, then here's some data on bridges that might whet their appetites.

1. The solid foundations that rest on the land on either side of the bridge are called the *abutments*. The columns in between that reach down into the water and into bedrock are called the *piers*. They usually have steel *collars* or *cutwaters* around them to keep them from damage or being eroded by water.

2. The bridge builders who worked below the water were sealed in *caissons*—watertight boxes or cylinders with controlled air pressure, like little houses or like underwater space capsules. Sometimes caissons stay underwater, and once the work is finished, they're filled with concrete and become the base for a pier.

3. After the foundation is built, the superstructure and the

road can be added in many possible ways. Sometimes they hang the cables and then work the road in from either end, or sometimes they float out the pieces of the road on barges and then raise them right into position.

4. The most exciting of modern bridges are *suspension bridges,* which can span great distances. First the foundation is built, then two huge towers. The towers support the approaches and also the cables, which loop down (like double-dutch ropes) and rise again to the tower on the other side. The cables start in anchorings on land and are like strings pulled tight and back on either side of the structure to help keep the bridge up.

5. There are also movable bridges. Kids love drawbridges (officially called *bascule bridges—bascule* means "seesaw") that have *leaves* that open and raise. But in many cities, you can find other types of movable bridges, including the kind where the roadway itself can be raised and lowered to allow a ship to pass under, and swing bridges, which have wheels that turn the middle part of the bridge open at a right angle (like a door).

To find the different types of bridges in your area, contact your local bridge (or bridge and tunnel) authority, transportation department, or port authority. These agencies usually have very large community relations or publicity departments—after all, their job is to get business for your city's ports and seaways. They can also tell you which bridges are under repair and reconstruction—equally interesting to watch.

### Enjoying the City's Architecture With Kids

Kids may not be turned on by studying a building or its history. But in fact they are fascinated by the structures themselves. One very enjoyable and well recommended parent/kid pastime in the city is taking a sketch pad, finding an office terrace or an outdoor table at a restaurant, and drawing a city building. Any building will really do, but if you're interested

If your city has a port or harbor, your child can learn a lot about boats and bridge construction, while enjoying a natural surrounding. (PHOTO BY WILLA ZAKIN)

in finding unusual or historical buildings, call your local historical society (for the old) and your local chapter of the American Institute for Architects (for the new). Kids between the ages of eight and twelve particularly enjoy these outings. Pencil sketching is easiest, but you can also photograph a building, a church, a piece of park sculpture, or a modern playground slide; then develop the photos, and try to reproduce them as sculptures at home. The main thing is not the art but the outing—the walking together and the lunch at some open air café opposite a building you want to sketch.

## Excavation, Archeology, and City History

Most people think of archeology and artifact hunting as a faraway or, at best, a countryside activity. But artifact hunting can be fabulous fun in a city. Artifacts are simply objects people have made throughout history that archeologists study to learn about man's behavior. And there are no greater sources of artifacts than certain city sites, such as urban renewal areas, excavations (for example, where a road is being widened or a building constructed), and the riverbanks that run right through the middle of many of our cities. Modern artifacts, of course, surround us—everything that is abandoned, from couches to TVs, video games, and computers that have gone out of style—and kids often are instinctively junk collectors. But that feeling of digging, of finding the hidden, can be enjoyed anywhere in a city. This is detective work and exploring together at its most fun. It's also collecting, which kids from eight years of age and up get a great deal of pleasure from.

How to start?

Take a walk along your city's riverbanks, around any dirt pile or grassy area (there are many of these in even the most built-up city), or around an excavation or a construction site (carefully, obviously). Use a walking stick with a sharpened point to turn over stones, a pocketknife to expose tips of rocks that might be interesting, and don't forget a knapsack for holding possible specimens. And if you're really into it, a metal detector for post-Indian relics can be very helpful and fun. The borders of our cities near river edges, or where roads have cut into natural rock, are great places to look. If you're exploring alone, bring along a book such as McHargue's and Roberts's *A Field Guide to Conservation Archeology in North America* (New York: Lippincott, 1977) or Michael Hudoba's *The Artifact Hunter's Handbook* (Chicago: Contemporary Books, 1979). These books list what to look for in your area.

In many cities these days, the Environmental Protection Act demands that an archeologist investigate any construction site. If they have reason to believe, for example, that there's an ancient burial ground beneath a proposed building, law requires that they explore the location. If you call your local museum of natural history, or the state archeologist's office (most capital cities have a state archeologist!), the local archeology department of a university, or the local historical society, you'll discover what areas they've been sent out to check and just where exploration is taking place—and even if you can assist them. In Rochester, for example, high school students assisted in two burial site explorations in the last ten years. And, says one parent, "If you find the site while they're working, they're more likely to let you help or just go-fer than if you call them on the phone." Showing interest by showing up often does the trick. Even if they won't allow you to help, you can watch them work.

On your own, keep an eye out for urban renewal work in the old parts of your city. Old houses with basements made of earth are great archeological resources. People in Colonial times didn't have trash compacters and tended to throw the trash in corners of the basement and bury it. When a bulldozer excavates an old neighborhood, tearing down old houses, these trash treasures are often found. In fact, several years ago, in Baltimore, where some basement artifact hunting revealed a Colonial iron lock and some old toys and coins, basement digging became the rage. And several years ago, in Alexandria, Virginia, when construction of a new courthouse was about to begin in an old, deteriorated section of town—a section that had once been a thriving commercial area—and the local archeological commission began a dig, at every layer they found the objects of people who lived on that city block at different periods.

Finally, of course, more modern artifacts can be found everywhere—on the sidewalks, in empty lots, and so on. Old bottles, grocery boxes, toys, posters, and even furniture and paintings, are becoming history every day.

## Trips to New Neighborhoods

In a city like New York, you could spend your entire youth exploring the new neighborhoods settled by different ethnic or immigrant groups—and when you'd finished, the neighborhoods would have changed and you'd have to start again. In most large cities, there are a host of places to bike to—not just pretty country scenes outside the city, but the financial district on a Sunday, the wholesale food markets, the ports, and the various ethnic neighborhoods. Taking an all-day bike ride to a place you've never been or taking one of the buses you've never ridden and getting off at the last stop—if you're at all nervous, ask the bus driver where the last stop is and if you'd be safe there—are just two of the spontaneous activities that make city life continually surprising. They do take courage but in fact there's little to worry about, say most of the adventurers we spoke to.

Once you get to a new neighborhood, trying an ethnic restaurant with a sense of adventure may result in your kid's actually eating things he would say "Yuck" to at home. Bring home some of the local produce, fish, spices, cheeses, and make dinner together. Talk to the store owners, if they speak English. Ask them how to say "Hello," "Good-bye," and "How are you?" in whatever language they speak. Take in the sights and the smells and, most of all, people-watch. Watch how they handle their kids, their mates, and their customers. See if you can find a neighborhood that's Russian—or Thai, Jewish, Vietnamese, Korean, Chinese, Japanese, and so on. Almost every big city has them. Biking, especially for active kids, makes the adventure more physical and satisfying for everyone. Says one New York teenager, "When I was eight or nine, my dad and I used to go on all-day bike rides. All I cared about was biking farther than the last time, and tasting whatever that neighborhood's equivalent of a hot dog was—souvlaki, chow mein, kielbasa, sausage. I had junk food in seven languages. It was great! Dad thought I was actually learning by having junk food! That's definitely one way to keep adults and kids happy at the same time."

## Exploring a City Port and Its Piers

Most cities have ports and piers to explore, and they can be fascinating and a bit awesome to any young child—especially if you look closely and try to identify the ships that arrive. It's fun to go down to the piers with a child, and many parents particularly recommend this adventure as an ideal time to take a camera and go photographing together. Many kids take endless pleasure in watching things move on conveyer belts; and since a pier is basically a place for packing and unpacking, they spend many happy hours watching objects get loaded, hoisted, shifted, and dropped.

A good basic book about piers is Paul C. Scotti's *Seaports: Ships, Piers, and People* (New York: Julian Messner, 1980). Another is *Harbor Tug*, by Peter Burchard and Rollie McKenna (New York: Putnam, 1975), which describes the ports of New York and New Jersey and the role of tugboats there. Here are some things to find out:

1. Does your city have a natural deep harbor, like New York's and San Diego's, or was it dug and deepened, like Houston's and Buffalo's? How deep is the harbor? If there are barges far out in the harbor emptying the loads of medium-size tankers or small tankers before they come into port, the harbor is probably not that deep.
2. What kind of ships dock there? Some modern vessels to keep an eye out for are various types of container ships (ones that house huge containers and railroad cars of merchandise, instead of storing crates and bags of produce individually). There are three kinds of container ships: *Vanships* contain huge aluminum or steel boxcars that were transported on the back of trucks or as railroad freight cars. You can spot a vanship because it often has containers stacked right on the main deck. *Lashes* are barges that store smaller barges, which in turn store containers that are being transferred to larger ships! *Ro-Ros* are ships that cars, farm machinery, and construction equipment roll on and off of. Eight-to-ten-year-olds love them.

You can also spot, of course, sailboats, navy ships, tankers, ferries, police boats, fire boats, fishing boats, and yachts.

3. What goes on in the port itself? A lot of the loading and unloading there can fascinate kids. There may be grain terminals, huge silos near the water. A ship anchors nearby and the grain is run through long tubes into cargo holds. Look for tank farms, where liquid cargos move through pipes and hoses to ships. And, most familiar, there will probably be container terminals, like huge parking lots that have hundreds of containers waiting to be picked up by boats or trucks. Near them you'll notice huge *straddle carriers*—a kind of truck that can take a container and move it to the waterfront, piling them three high as they wait to be loaded.

4. Who does the work? Look for the stevedores, who load and unload the ships.

5. Can you tour the harbor by boat? Check with your local port authority for schedules.

Exploring the city together in an unstructured, simple manner is a wonderful way to be together with your children, to build confidence in and familiarity with their environment, and to have fun. It can also result in less worry when your city kids get older and go out on their own. One mother of a Manhattan teenager said, "My son learned to explore when he was little. Little kids explore in the country. They explore grass and trees. How can you compare that to what a teenager explores here— life, neighborhoods? Not long ago, my son got a gift of some money and he wanted to buy something. If he'd lived in the country, he would have gone with his friends in a car to shop.

Instead, he decided to go to the Lower East Side where the hip clothing stores are. He was exploring, by himself, a whole part of the city—people, experiences, events, uniqueness, individuality."

# INFORMAL INTRODUCTIONS: CULTURAL LIFE

*I* let my son take along a book (to concerts). I know that's taboo, but I let him read when he's bored. Then when a moment comes up that's great, I nudge him and he listens. You know you can listen to a minute or two of a fun piece, just like you can listen to a popular song. It takes a while to build an attention span. It's hard work.

—A mother, Rochester, N.Y.

*W*hen I was growing up on Long Island, museums could have been on Mars. True, we made occasional forays into Manhattan to the huge, dark halls of the Planetarium or the Museum of Natural History. We were urged by teachers to stare at awesome display cases; we took notes; but basically we knew it was a day teachers didn't have to teach, and therefore kids wouldn't have to do homework. So I, like many suburban kids, grew up museumless and, you might say, artless.

—Janet G., Queens, N.Y.

*Artless* is not such a terrific thing to be—because art, knowledge, sophistication, and creativity mean emotional and intellectual freedom. The arts are one of the greatest gifts we can give our city kids.

It's important, said many parents of children who love museums and concerts and theater, not to think of museums and concert halls as intimidating cultural centers but as places, like other places, to play, to be stimulated, to have fun—in a different way from on a ballfield, certainly, and following different rules, definitely, but still to have fun. Kids let loose to enjoy museums *will* enjoy them.

Said one New York father, "To me, art was something kids drew and fine art was boring to them. But when my son was three years old, we were supposed to meet my wife at the Autopub. We were early and near the Metropolitan. We wandered around and then stood in front of a Jackson Pollock painting because that's where he seemed to want to stand. And I just asked, 'Do you like it?' And he said, 'Yes,' and I asked why. And he said—and I swear this is true—'I like it cause it's free, it moves around. It's like the wind blowing leaves.' That's when I looked at the title of the painting. It was called *Autumn Rhythm*. Not only did the museum turn into a great way for me to share time with my kid, but I learned something—that kids at that age see a lot like artists. And that each moment is like no other childhood moment—if you don't catch it then, you'll miss it forever. Four months later I took him to see that painting again. What did he think it was about? 'I don't know, it's a mess,' he said. 'I like it, but it's a mess.'"

Parents who've ventured into museums with very small children told us stories of moments just like that one—special moments, funny moments, or moments of insight for parent or child. Of course, we also heard stories of cranky babies and guards who take your strollers and then can't seem to find them when you want them back. But the chances for a successful afternoon at a museum are just about the same as any other place that you attend with little kids. It will be worse only if you're intimidated by the institutional quality of the place or if you're intent on "improving" and educating your child. Wherever you go, kids will be kids—but if you prepare for a museum in the right way and are prepared to depart if the day is not working out, you're likely to love it and you're likely to give children something they can enjoy right through adolescence, with or without you. One young adolescent friend of ours, a sensitive, sweet, kind punk rocker, hangs out at the Boston Museum of Fine Arts. She grew up there, visiting it regularly with her mom, in a relaxed way—what she calls a "We got nothing to do today, so you want to go to the movies or the museum? kind of way." Now seventeen, she says, "I love it there. It's like a home to me. I walk. I have this one gallery I write my songs in. It's very comforting to be there, to be alone, to think, surrounded by such beautiful things. And a lot of these guys who painted here seem like they were just like me."

## HOW TO SHARE A MUSEUM WITH YOUR KIDS

Randy Williams and Susan Springer, associate directors of education of the Metropolitan Museum in New York, suggest that there are ways to enjoy art with kids of every age, making it part of their childhood.

### FOUR- TO SEVEN-YEAR-OLDS

First of all, you want your children to like the museum. You want them to feel at home there, not intimidated and not uncomfortable. So dress comfortably, with comfortable shoes for you. Check your coats, your paraphernalia, your other stuff at the coat-check counter, but bring a couple of toys along so that your little kids can play. (Make them quiet toys, of course; but there's nothing wrong with sitting on a gallery floor doing a puzzle or putting shapes in holes.) If you're not intimidated by the place, they won't be.

Secondly, since you're going to relax at the museum, it's always better to go when it's not crowded. If you aren't working or if it's your day off, go in late afternoon. Between three and five, museums tend to be empty or else loaded with other kids. Avoid weekends, especially Sundays.

Thirdly, plan to stay about a half an hour to an hour. As in show business, with museums it's always best to leave your kids wanting more. Williams suggests that you take little kids to just one room or gallery for each trip. You can let them wander until they get to a place they like. As Williams, who has developed a real reputation for getting New York City students to love museums and art, says, "I take my two sons, Kenyatta, six, and Justin, four. I tell them that one object is theirs, that they should each go around and pick out the one object that's theirs. Then they get to talk about it for as long as they like. I also make one object mine—that way we *all* get to interrupt each other. The other day we went to the Michael Rockefeller wing of the Metropolitan. Kenyatta picked out a buffalo. Justin found a mask with heads on the front and the back. He started talking and said it reminded him of Florida. It looked just like an alligator to him. And, you know what? When I looked closely at the elongated shape, it was an alligator. He had made the connection before I did."

"Bestowing" an object on your toddler or selecting a room that's especially yours and hers seems to produce an attachment and loyalty to those objects. Kids love to own things, to identify things as their favorites—and even to hate the objects that aren't theirs. Let them wander around and pick out something that's the ugliest thing they ever saw.

What exhibits are perfect for little kids? Primitive art, abstract art, pop art, sculpture of any kind. Bright colors. Pollock. Stella. Red Grooms. Oldenburg. Extremes. Big things, and incredibly little, detailed things. Illuminated manuscripts seem to appeal to some kids the way those tiny two-inch books and ceramic sculptures do.

### EIGHT- TO TWELVE-YEAR-OLDS

This is an even easier age to take kids to museums. They're not a drag to take on the bus; they won't get cranky for a bottle; they just like being with you. It's the perfect age to start bringing along a sketch book—for yourself as well as one for them.

(No one minds if you sketch in a museum.) But remember, these are the years when they like facts and specifics, and they resent being told what to think. They decide what's good and bad, they love and hate things on their own, and being told something's "great art" doesn't cut it. Just enjoy and share the time together.

Here are some objects and artists they're bound to like to spend an hour with:

*THE IMPRESSIONISTS.* Kids seem to love them. They like to sketch them, and there's a sense as your browse, even though you're in a museum, that you're outside. If you need or want to help kids understand what they see, you can ask, "Do you feel the sun in the painting?" or "What kind of day does it look like in there?" Try to relate the art to what your kids are currently interested in, says Springer. For example, with a six- or seven-year-old who's learning about time and days, you might ask at, say, Monet's *Boating,* whether she can figure out what day it is in the painting. ("Remember, it was the old days, when they worked every day but one. Are they working now?")

*RED GROOMS.* Everybody enjoys him.

*THE EGYPTIAN EXHIBITS.* "They liked it before *Raiders of the Lost Ark,*" says Randy Williams, referring to New York's Metropolitan collection, of course. "Now they love it." It has, he adds, the wonderful quality of being from the past but seeming like the future to them. "Especially the hieroglyphics. There are two types of hieroglyphics—the pictorial and the symbolic type—and kids love to decode the latter. For example, a typical hieroglyphic might be a hippopotamus with lotus flower. You can have them come up with their favorite animal, come up with their favorite flower, and go home and draw that flower inside that animal."

*CLAES OLDENBURG.* Kids tend to love his inflatables, his mouse museum, his ray gun museum, and other pieces.

*THE SURREALISTS.* Dali, Tanguy, and the others intrigue kids.

*PICASSO.* Although abstract art is not the eight- to twelve-year-old's strong suit, Picasso squeaks by, especially his sculptures and early art.

On the negative side, Susan Springer and Randy Williams find that Greek art and statues seem to bore kids and often embarrass them.

Another fun thing to do with these kids is to visit the museum gift shop. Just as kids collect baseball cards, they can begin to collect slides or postcards.

There are many other ways to give kids art. They are, of course, usually into creating their own art. They tend to love certain cartoonists, illustration art, and even advertising art. Many cities have an education center at the local art museum or natural history museum that will have exhibits geared to those interests. And that museum will also know the names of local artists. Randy Williams urges parents to find local artists and to try to arrange a visit to the studio of one who has—or likes!—kids. Perhaps even a small fee can be arranged. Seeing a real artist work, he says, will add a dimension to those museum visits. Anything you do to make art more human, more personal, more honest, to help kids understand the urge behind the painting and make it seem less formal, is a gift to your kids.

## MUSIC AND DANCE CONCERTS

Like art, music not only can enrich anyone's world, it can be a meaningful part of any family's life. There is always that image of the ideal family: They are not watching television; they are singing around a piano, playing chamber music together, even listening to records together, respecting each generation's favorite songs. If music is a universal language, it is also a language that can ease communications in any home. As composer Lester Trimble said, "How can good music not bring people closer? You feel a sense of kinship by just listening. Sharing and witnessing anything great with anyone—and certainly a relative—is an intimate moment." And, he added, "Ideally, you value listening to music as you value listening to each other."

It has been our discovery, unfortunately, after speaking to many musicians, composers, music or dance teachers, and (especially) parents that "good" music is an area of tension and insecurity for many adults. If they're giving their children music lessons, they're often frustrated by fights about practicing. Some regret not playing enough "good" music in the home. Or if they take their kids to concerts, often the kids are bored.

Families can be the ideal forum for listening, reviving, and sharing good music and dance. Many American cities have fine orchestras with young people's concerts, young people's orchestras, family programs, fine dance groups, and excellent music and dance teachers. The resources are there. There are many ways to integrate them successfully into your family's life. Here are a few suggestions:

1. First, listen and watch at home. TV is a wonderful free introduction to symphonic music, ballet, jazz, and opera. The *Live from Lincoln Center* concerts, for example, on public television are a great beginning for kids. As one twelve-year-old young man who had never been to a live

concert said, as he sat watching the expressive Itzhak Perlman play Sarasate's *Carmen Fantasy* during the premier philharmonic concert last year, "He's good. I wouldn't mind seeing him in person. Of course, I don't own a tuxedo."

Television, with its closeups of both instruments and faces, is a wonderful start for kids. They can also talk and ask questions, and when they get bored, they can turn it off.

2. Nancy Hager, a professor of music at Brooklyn College, suggests attending any free or outdoor concerts with kids. Walk around, circulate, watch concerts in the parks, or stop and listen to street musicians—student violinists, reggae bands, rock groups, or jazz musicians. Said one mother, "I don't know what it is about stopping alone, but I usually don't. I have this weird resistance to it. But now, when I'm with my son, who's three, I force myself because I see his wonder. Also, he just loves to put a quarter in someone's hat. He'll listen, he'll dance, and I realize what I was missing."

3. Listen to music in places your kids enjoy going to for other reasons. A natural history museum, for example, will always have some music as part of various children's programs. Kids shows will often feature dance, as well.

4. Go to half a concert. Formal concerts, even young people's concerts, are tough for many smaller kids to sit through. So, when you think there's something your child might enjoy or that you love and would love to share, make sure you don't mind leaving. There is nothing wrong, says Nancy Hager, with "selective listening"— even in person.

5. When you do start attending concerts, remember that you

171

can take a child to almost any kind of music event if you give him the appropriate background and help him with things to listen for. Says Hager, "Many of us are impatient with our children being bored...but we don't offer them the tools to prevent boredom." Research the program a little beforehand, if only to read the notes on the back of a record or to skim the concert program. Talk about the performance to come.

As one mother said, "I took my seven-year-old to a chamber music concert, and I was dreading it. We play music at home, but we're not total devotees. So, before the concert started, an all-Haydn concert, in fact, I just told him that what he was going to hear was a conversation, just like people talking. The first violin was going to say something interesting—that's called the theme. And then the other instruments, which have different sounds, like different people, are going to respond. Someone may pick up the theme and say it differently, and the other two instruments will just sit and listen—you can see how they're facing each other. Sometimes they even give a funny answer—it was a structure. It really helped. And all night he kept saying 'I think that part was funny...' He listened. And he loved it."

6. Appreciating music and dance depends on taste, so don't prejudice them. Not every musical piece or dance appeals to everyone. Many of us are raised with a lack of what Michelle Audette of the New York City Ballet calls "cultural confidence." She says, "We think that there's one right way of seeing, hearing, and evaluating art. And there isn't. It's fun to see, hear, and disagree." Let kids talk about what they feel and whether they like whatever they're hearing or seeing. In fact, especially in that middle

age of strong opinions, of no grays—eight to twelve—
just go with it. Your kids will be subtler and more analyti-
cal later on.

After a concert or ballet, Audette recommends asking
questions such as: "What do you remember most?"
"What color do you think of when you think of that part of
the program?" "What do you think it would feel like if you
were the ballerina (or violinist or conductor) on stage?"
"How did it make your skin feel?" "What part did you
hate or what part was boring?" "How did that make your
eyes feel?"

7. If your child loves the performance, go backstage. You'd
be surprised how many artists will talk to kids or give au-
tographs. Send a note back beforehand if necessary. It
can amount to nothing, but it can just as likely lead to a
wonderful, serendipitous moment. If you can't go backstage, you can send away for an autographed picture or
write a fan letter to an artist through the record company.
Many artists respond.

8. Become involved with your children's school and its art,
music, and theater programs. If the school doesn't have
these programs, find out whether the local city orchestra
and dance groups sponsor programs in the schools. If
you can, attend those concerts with your kids and encourage other parents to. You'll enjoy them, and you can
learn a lot together.

If your child's school is not using available art or music
programs, find out why. Many private schools have excellent music and art programs of their own but are un-
aware that they are eligible for certain free concerts. Or,
in the public schools, programs could be limited by
money. Find out how much it costs to bring the orchestra

to your school. If the parents' association can't afford to sponsor it, there are often grants available to help.

To find out about available music and dance concerts, whether free or especially geared to kids and families, call your city's cultural affairs department, orchestra, or ballet company; or try your state arts council.

In a big city, if you're busy, employed, or following other interests with your kids, you can consider a simpler but valuable alternative. When you talk about your kid's day, ask not just about the main subjects but also about music and art classes. Talk about them together. Talk to the teachers and ask if there's any way to get a list of featured pieces so that you might purchase a recording of what your child loved. If there's an interested parent who does attend school performances, he or she can even make a list of what music or dance various kids liked most.

## THEATER

Theater, for many of us, is the most easily accessible of all the arts. We take our little kids to see musicals, puppet shows, and plays for children. David Shookhoff, a national consultant in theater arts education, believes our kids can also enjoy and appreciate so much more—not just new plays, but especially revivals of the classics, from Shakespeare for little kids to Moliere and to Tennessee Williams for older ones.

"In some ways, children are far less critical than adults," he maintains. "They have a different sensibility. (There's probably an aesthetic developmental process, like there is cognitive and moral development). At young ages, for at least short periods of times, children are just enthralled by theater being live, by it being colorful and dramatic and real." You have to take some risks, Shookhoff believes, "But it's worth it. They often like more than you do!"

Like all the other arts, the more difficult the material, the more you want to prepare your kids in advance. If you're going to see a popular modern musical, you may not have to do anything in advance. But if you're going to see a Shakespearean comedy, you should. And it isn't that difficult. Find a way to engage your child's imagination beforehand, to have her wrestle with the central issue of the play or story before she goes, so that she (in a way) is in the same mindset as the playwright.

For example, say you're about to take your child to *A Comedy of Errors,* a great play for kids. You might say to your seven-year-old, "What would happen if a pair of identical twins showed up in a small town, and each didn't even know the other existed and certainly didn't know the other was going around this very town? And, say, one was a married twin, so that when the twin's wife saw the other twin, she got confused? What are some of the things that could happen?"

*Twelfth Night?* You might ask, "What if a girl was disguised as a guy and you really couldn't tell she was a girl *at all?* And then what if another girl didn't know the guy was a girl, and the girl fell in love with her?"

Or *The Glass Menagerie,* by Tennessee Williams, or *Our Town,* by Thornton Wilder. Or *Room Service,* by John Murray and Allen Boretz; or Moliere's *The Doctor in Spite of Himself* or *The Miser.* There are "what ifs" for all of them, a few central, down-to-earth questions. Essentially, we're talking about finding the dramatic situation in each story and expressing it in a way that will intrigue your child. You might even read a scene with them, especially a difficult one.

Whether it's San Francisco's Act, the Seattle Rep, Minneapolis's Guthrie Theatre, or Rochester's G.E.V.A., most cities now have excellent companies that put on one or two of these revivals a year. Many of them put on special performances for schools, but going with your child is even better. It's fun for the whole family, and it's the most individualized instruction a child can get. You know your children best and you know how best to engage their imaginations.

Don't be *too* concerned, say many adults, parents, and theater lovers, about protecting your child from some aspect of the play. Said one parent, "I remember my mother taking me to see *King Lear* because they wanted to see it and couldn't get a babysitter; they kept warning my brother and me that his eyes would be gouged out at the end—and don't be scared. I remember that, sure, but I remember so much more. I was so glad I saw it, I loved it." Or, said another, "My parents took me to *Pirates of Penzance* when I was six. They kept telling me it was about babies being switched—but don't worry, it would never happen to me. I'm sure it's about other things, but all I remember is that *Pirates of Penzance* was about switched babies. They should have at least waited till after I saw it to see if I even noticed."

Some productions will be boring, some exciting. No one production will turn off your kid to Shakespeare or to any theater permanently, so take some risks. One mother recalls taking her nine-year-old to a production of *A Midsummer Night's Dream* performed by Shakespeare on the Mount in Lenox, Massachusetts. The play was performed outdoors on a summer evening, while the audience picnicked and watched scenes that took place at the edge of real woods and on the balconies of a grand estate. It was enthralling, funny, colorful, spectacular. So much so that her son said at the conclusion of his first Shakespearean play, "That was so great. They ought to put this guy on Broadway!"

Finally, keep in mind that one of the best forms of theater to take your kids to is opera. Yes, it really is. Most opera repertory companies perform one or two operas in English, and many now provide supertitles to help with the language barrier. If kids can see *Madama Butterfly, The Barber of Seville,* or *La Boheme,* they'll love it. After all, we're talking about splendid productions, stories that are basic and direct, and actors that sing exactly what they feel. These are passionate stories with soap opera elements, and if kids can enjoy *All My Children,* they can enjoy *Madama Butterfly.*

You can prepare for this kind of performance as for any other theatrical experience. You can tell your kids the story beforehand, you can act it out, you can listen to some of the music—all ways to engage your children in the main issues of the story. David Shookhoff, for example, took a group of twelve-year-old city kids to *Madama Butterfly.* First he gave them a description of the story. He talked a little about ideas such as betrayal or leaving someone behind, about being an unwed parent, about a father leaving a family and then coming back. They weren't bored. They could relate very well to that story. And they watched and listened, engrossed—so engrossed, in fact, that, in the last act, when Pinkerton returns, these kids booed him!

Which gets us back to our initial premise: The arts, all the arts, are not only entertaining but as enriching and helpful and enlightening and provocative to children as they are to adults—and one of the strongest reasons it can be wonderful to be a city family.

# NATURAL RESOURCES

*I* was no wiseacre or particularly streetwise Philistine. I was timid and insecure, but I knew exactly what I wanted to do as an adult. I would study dinosaurs, a firm conviction inspired by one supreme moment of childhood terror dissipated by fascination— my first look at *Tyrannosaurus rex* in the American Museum of Natural History.

—Stephen Jay Gould★

*I* love the city. And even when I get away and go to the seashore or the country, I think I even appreciate the ocean and stars and stuff more. As a city kid, I don't ever take it for granted.

—Dahlia R., Cambridge, Massachusetts, age fifteen

★*New York Times Book Review* (August 13, 1986):36.

*W*e spend summers in Northern Vermont. You do have to get into the country in the summer. My mom tells this story about when I was eight. We went to the country store for the first time and we got farm fresh eggs. And we took them home and we cracked them, and they were so great—fresh, and all double yolked. And I was amazed, and Mom looked at me and said, "Amazing, right?" And I said, "Yeah! I thought you could only get double yolk eggs in Zabars!"*

Sarah P., New York City, age thirteen

Just as we know that a visiting child can't know the city, feel its energy and identity without living in it, so we know that you can't be a country kid, Nature's child, in the city. But your children can still grow up with a love of nature and a sense of being comfortable in it. Many city kids do. Said one city father, "I grew up in the suburbs, and although it's true I experienced the seasons more fully, nature was not an important part of my life. I practically never saw a large animal there. I wasn't looking. My parents thought nature was just a place that got you dirty. Now I live with my kids in Manhattan. They spend summers in the country, we go camping and fishing and skiing, we have cats and a dog, we had a lizard, a neurotic gerbil; my kids belonged to Zoo Kids and Campfire Girls; we even found a garter snake in

*The famous food store in New York City, where you can find almost anything.

Central Park that we kept as a pet and named The Mayor. I know they have a greater sense of nature's power and beauty than I ever did. I think city parents can give kids a lot of the country if they want to."

Although many city parents leave the city to look for nature, there is an extraordinary degree to which nature is part of our daily lives: in our parks, in city lakes and ponds, or in our backyard. Nature on the city streets means ants and insects and pigeons and squirrels, as well as hardy city trees and lovingly planted community flower gardens. There are animals, too, such as raccoons, foxes, armadillos, and oppossums roaming free in our parks. Hundreds of species of birds have been spotted in the parks of our busiest cities. Then, of course, the most amazing animals live in our cities' zoos; the most amazing plants grow in our botanical gardens.

These mothers got together and took their children to the Bronx Zoo. Outings with friends or family can be fun for adults as well as kids. Check with your local zoo for special family programs. (PHOTO BY LESLIE FELDMAN)

181

## THE BEST APPROACH

Find a group of kids and parents and go for a walk or picnic in a park, roam the dunes at the nearby seashore, or just stroll a city street. When you find a suitable spot, have one parent define the boundaries, and watch that those safe borders are upheld; then send the other parents off to explore with the kids.

Dorothy Shuttlesworth, author of *Exploring Nature with Your Child* (New York: Abrams, 1977) urges parents not to overwhelm their kids with facts. They are exploring what it means to be outside, to run loose, to feel free, and to make discoveries. "Information is invaluable," she says, "but we must pass it on in such a way that we do not overwhelm the child's own modest discoveries. . . . On the whole, the successful approach lies in encouraging inquisitiveness and providing opportunities to satisfy curiosity."

For a child to really see, however, he does need a little help. A "Look at this" is often necessary because a three- or four-year-old can pass through a field of wildflowers, trees, and birds and see only one thing: another toddler's toy. Even older kids are often bent on racing to the top of a hill, passing interesting things as they do. Said one nature enthusiast, a city boy scout leader for thirty years, "There's nothing like stopping a stampeding herd of ten-year-olds with a 'Say, what's this?" and then pull out from the earth an Indian cucumber, wash it, and eat it." He advises parents, "You need to plan a little, but your plan is to heighten the chances of one thing—surprise, because surprise is the key to loving nature. That's why so many kids get bored by nature class. But let them wander into a park clearing on a summer day and spot a garter snake sunning on a rock—and they're yours. A country kid experiences nature as spontaneous, but with a bit of adult help, so can a city kid."

## NATURE IN A CITY PARK

Here are some easy and fun ways, suggested by veteran city parents, to help kids enjoy nature in their city parks. They can be adapted for almost any age, from toddler on up to teen:

1. Adopt a tree. One mother took her son exploring in the neighborhood park when he was three. They adopted a favorite tree, a large oak. It became "their" tree. "When he was three, he would hug and kiss it, or we followed its roots. When he was four, he looked at its leaves, bark, and flowers; he visited it each season to see how it changed. When he was seven and eight, he played ball near it. When he was nine, it's where he buried his pet gerbil. Now that he's thirteen, we'll go and talk there sometimes. We found that tree by accident, but he was as attached to it as any country boy to his back meadow."

You can just enjoy your tree, or you can learn some basic lessons from it. For example, you can follow the roots and talk about how they bring up food and water, or discuss why the leaves are green. You can identify the tree—look at the bark and the shape of its leaves and find them in a simple tree identification book. See what birds seem to visit it and what animals hang around it. Climb it. Picnic under it. Have a birthday party around it.

Come back periodically and observe the tree change from season to season. This is a great opportunity to talk about cycles and change, as well as about growth and growing up.

2. Adopt a territory. Just as with the tree, pick a small area in the park or at the pond or beach that you can follow from season to season. Study it. Mark off your territory with some private code—a painted rock at each border, for example. Within your territory, the kids can dig and can pretend to find fossils of dinosaurs; your seven-year-old can begin a mineral collection, a twig collection, a berry collection. If you're really into it, you can keep a record of the animals and birds that you observe, of animal tracks, of a new wildflower that's begun to grow there. You and your child can paste souvenirs and notes in a picture book, or keep a diary.

3. Watch birds. Even toddlers love birds, and at the age of three and four can learn to identify a robin or a sparrow or a bluejay. If they're really interested, take along a simple bird book (see the bibliography). Look up a particular bird or two that's likely to cross their paths—a cardinal, a tanager, a chickadee, or oriole, for example—and then take a walk to see if you can spot it.

When you do spot that bird, it's fun for all kids to learn to "stalk it." Teach them to imitate a cat and tiptoe slowly and quietly near the bird—and come back with the answers to these questions, which will train them to be fledgling birders:

- "How big is the bird compared to a bird you know— say, a robin or a pigeon?"
- "What seems special about the way that bird looks? Does it have a special feature—a funny-colored beak or band around its neck or an interesting tail?"

- "How does the bird walk? With one foot in front of the other? Does it hop?"
- "What color are its feathers?"
- "What color beak does it have? What kind of beak?"
- "What did its wings look like when it flew away?"

If they can answer any of these questions, they've begun to learn bird identification and can probably begin to use a simple bird book. Said one mother, "I got my daughter simple binoculars and we went to the park with an Audubon Society walking tour. For the first half hour, they'd spot a bird, yell 'Scarlet tanager at twelve o'clock' at some tree, and everyone would aim their binoculars at it. And we'd still be focusing. When they said, 'Everybody spot that bird?' we'd see nothing, but we'd lie, say yes, look at each other, and giggle. We didn't want to hold up the crowd. That first time we saw nothing, but we felt real close. Now, at the turn of spring every year, we go out with a Peterson guidebook and look. Our goal is to be together and to have fun outdoors, to be birders and not teenager and mother. It always brings us closer, at least for the time we do it."

If you're going to birdwatch in a city park, stick to the familiar paths—you're bound to find birds to excite you, as well as other people, to feel safe. The best binoculars to start with is the simple seven or eight-power glass with a center focus screw so you can focus both eyes at the same time. Go out and practice using the binoculars first. They do take some time getting used to, both for adults and children.

4. Hunt for nests. One father of a brood of three youngsters under ten spends the first days of a dismal city winter in

the park searching for nests. They're a whole lot easier to spot when the trees are bare. And they're exciting for a kid. With a guidebook, you can identify a nest and figure out what kind of bird built it—and the next spring, return and find either that same mother bird or at least that same species rebuilding.

5. Watch, catch, and collect animals. Call your local park rangers, the Audubon Society, the natural history or science museum and ask them what animals, from squirrels to foxes to frogs, have been spotted in your city's parks. Ask them where the snakes tend to sun themselves; where an overturned rock might yield some crawly life; where the salamanders hang out. (It's easy to find a salamander: Just take a child along.) Then, with that little bit of research and planning, take your kids to the designated spot and wait for the surprise.

6. Follow the monarch from caterpillar to butterfly. If there's any nearby park area with milkweed, you're bound to find a monarch caterpillar around August. They're black, yellow, white, and green striped. Take it home with some of the milkweed, put it in a big jar with holes, and it will create a beautiful pale green chrysalis. In a few weeks, a monarch butterfly will emerge. The luna moth, truly one of the most beautiful of nature's flying creatures, is also fun to search for in caterpillar and cocoon stage.

7. Collect rocks, seeds, ants, or anything else. Collecting things will make a seven- to ten-year-old's day. Even bottlecap collecting in the park is fun, a way to explore— and clean—the park.

8. Play nature games (especially good for toddlers). Four-year-olds love Living Lotto. To play, scout an area, then

cut out pictures from magazines of natural objects or animals you know will be there. Then let your toddler find the real thing. Or, with a group, give each toddler a different picture and when they've all found their objects, they all win.

You can also play Close Your Eyes and Listen. Lie silently on the grass or a rock and try to identify the noises you and your child hear, whether it's the sound of the wind or a cricket or a squirrel scurrying up a tree. You can make this into more of a game if you close your eyes and give it a try, too. We hate to tell you who'll be better at it.

Alternate version is Close Your Eyes and Smell. In the city, especially for four-year-old boys, there'll be a lot of giggling.

9. Try geography games and orienteering. Kids get a kick out of hearing stories about what it was like when their city was still the country. Take out some library books on your town's history. Look at old pictures and then take a stroll through the park or the city streets to discover what those old places have become. Give older kids a compass and a map (get one from your local science museum or museum of natural history), and see if they can follow the route drawn on the map in order to reach a goal—say, the merry-go-round or the outdoor café or the site of an old farm. If you're worried about safety at all, split into groups of one adult and two kids.

Remember, too, for all of these activities, take a camera. These are some of the best action pictures you're going to take of your kids.

## SOME TIPS FOR KEEPING TODDLERS INTERESTED

- Ask questions as your kids look at things: "Why do you think that squirrel is burying that acorn?" "How did that pigeon see us and fly away when we were in back of him?"
- Play games, especially fantasy games. Whether kids learn anything or not, no matter where they are, they'll enjoy being there. The park can be a different planet or the place where E.T.'s uncle was spotted; it can be the jungle for the day or the North Pole, or any place the kids have fantasies about. Or each kid can pretend to be a park animal.
- Be physical. Be silly. Look at the trees upside down between your legs. Point to a sparrow and call it a moose. Kids will love to correct you. ("Are you *sure* that's not a moose?" say in astonishment. "What about that thing in the tree with the acorn in its mouth? Now, *that's* a moose! You're kidding? It's not?")
- Play hide and seek (in a confined area, of course).
- Give each child a little box (or have each decorate one beforehand) and let each one choose something to bring home. Toddlers can get into this and search and search for just the right thing.
- Read a book outdoors—a nature book, a nature tale, or any story. Again, outdoors is just a place to feel comfortable in.

## CITY ZOOS, BOTANICAL GARDENS, AND NATURE CENTERS

The zoos, botanical gardens, natural history museums, aquariums, and nature preserves in and around our cities are not only wonderful places to visit regularly with children: They also offer many special programs, camps, events, classes, and resources for kids and families.

To take advantage of natural resources in big cities, you have to plan. Like so many city institutions, zoos and natural history and science museums tend to be crowded, especially on weekends or when special children's events are listed in the local paper. Courses can be booked, too. If you want to find activities that are less well publicized or if you need to be reminded to sign up early for spring gardening, become a member of the nature centers that most interest you. The local natural history museum, zoo, and botanical gardens all seek your membership; and, in exchange, you'll get all their educational information, discounts, and schedules early. Becoming a member often offers your kids the opportunity for special and memorable treats. Said one mother, "I take my kid to the special lecture series for members of the New York Zoological Society. It's held at Lincoln Center. There are people with tuxedos in the audience, there are brilliant scientists who talk about elephants and how birds of paradise mate (and show slides) and there are fancy chandeliers above adorable animal exhibits in the lobby. No, it doesn't feel like the woods. But it's unique and it's great fun."

---

## FINDING NATURAL RESOURCES

---

If you need information about your city's resources, either call the education department of your local museum of natural history, state horticultural society, or local zoo; call the state department of parks and recreation or the local office of the U.S. Department of the Interior; or contact private organizations such as the National Wildlife Federation (8925 Leesburg Pike, Vienna, Virginia 22184), or the National Science for Youth Foundation (11 Wildwood Valley, NE, Atlanta, Georgia 30338; (404) 394–4350). This last organization publishes a directory of natural science centers and related facilities.

---

## ORGANIZED PROGRAMS

### The Zoo

Call your local zoo's education office and ask for information or brochures. There are usually four types of organized programs:

1. Zoo events—these are great but tend to be crowded. For example, many zoos run special days highlighting an exhibit or holiday programs for kids. The Bronx Zoo has two Halloween programs—one for little kids and one for over-sevens, in which they make masks, sing songs, tell stories, and visit the World of Darkness exhibit.
2. Extended children's programs—these include zoo clubs that meet one Saturday a month to talk about natural history or zoological topics, such as "What's a wildlife

190

biologist?" or "What's an endangered species?" There are also vacation programs. During your child's Christmas holiday, for example, your zoo might offer two- or three-day winter wildlife adventures that let kids visit the animals or cultures that survive in colder climates.

3. Summer camps—the Bronx Zoo offers a summer day camp, usually a week or two in length, that sends kids on a different "continental" journey each day. Perhaps they'll even get to be a keeper for a day, working in the pony barn or the children's zoo; get to ride a camel or an elephant; or go on a safari through Africa. Some zoos also offer an intern program for teenagers on animal care and maintenance.

4. Family programs—these can be great fun and are designed to be shared by you and your child. The whole family goes on treasure hunts or watches live animal demonstrations together, but parents also attend separate adult-oriented activities.

## Botanical Gardens or Arboretums

Many public gardens have instituted children's sections for kids ages nine and up who want to grow and harvest their own vegetables. In Brooklyn, where this idea began, kids sign up on a first-come-first-serve basis; in other cities, such as Cleveland, the program is run through schools. Fees are modest—at the Brooklyn Botanical Gardens, for example, the registration costs from $10 to $20; and kids are given a plot (four feet by fifteen feet for younger kids, eight feet by fifteen feet for teenagers), tools, seeds, and practical advice. They start with indoor classes on Saturdays and are out planting in May. Each child has a partner; and as Betsy Jacobs, associate director of education there, says, "It's really wonderful to see. There are

kids planting together from all the surrounding neighborhoods, kids from the wealthier brownstone families, kids from
Orthodox Jewish neighborhoods, Haitian kids, Hispanic kids,
lots of children from the West Indian neighborhood nearby.
They range from the very poor to the very wealthy, but it
doesn't matter—they're all in dungarees, they're all getting
their hands dirty. And they come back year after year as
friends."

Gardening programs are extremely popular. You may have
to call your local botanical garden in February to participate.
For a list of gardening centers and programs near you, contact
the National Gardening Association, 180 Flynn Avenue, Bur-
lington, Vermont, 05401 (802) 863–1308. If your local botanical garden or arboretum doesn't offer children's gardening,
check what else they offer. The Morris Arboretum in Philadelphia, for example, offers hayrides, leaf rubbings, and seasonal
festivals. And check with the local university extension service
or state horticultural society as well. They may also offer programs for urban gardeners, in which a whole family may get
involved. (University extension services now run 4-H clubs in
every major city of the country.)

### Nature Centers
Using a nature center directory, you can find nature centers or
wildlife sanctuaries specializing in a variety of children's programs (see the "Finding Natural Resources" box, page 190).
For example, the nature center in Milford, Pennsylvania, not
too far from Philadelphia, offers a solar center. The Schlitz
Audubon Center in Milwaukee offers an urban-environment
education program, with courses and curriculum on environmental problem solving. The Schuylkill Valley Nature Center

in Philadelphia has a bug house and a weather station. Many nature centers, such as Wave Hill in Riverdale, New York, offer bilingual programs for Spanish-speaking kids, too. Most have learning centers; pads to draw on; seasonal events; and chicks, beehives, or other sorts of live animal or science exhibits.

You can also call your city park or state conservation department for parks and wildlife refuges in your area, many of which offer programs for kids. Finally, join or ask to be placed on the National Audubon Society mailing list. The society runs over 175 sanctuaries. Some are closed to the public, some allow special visits by appointment only (with the warden, if he so deems, meeting you in a boat and showing you around), and some allow periodic visits.

### By the Beautiful Sea...or Aquarium
Call your local aquarium, the U.S. Department of the Interior's Fish and Game Department, or the national parks department to ask for information about their special programs for kids. These may include whale watching, free canoe instruction (through the Red Cross), fish hatchery tours, or fishing trips run by local YMCAs.

### Natural History Museums
And, of course, don't forget the great indoors: the natural history museums and nature exhibits at your local children's and science museums. Get on the mailing list. Become a member. You can find a listing of natural history, science and children's museums in your area by browsing through a directory put out by the American Association of Museums (at your library).

Call the museum's Education Department. Ask about hands-on exhibits, Discovery Rooms or People Centers, monthly festivals, and so on.

Ask if there's a special urban environment exhibit, a "nature in the city" program for kids. These exhibits display city animals, plants, and trees, the city's geological background; and cover some ecological and environmental issues.

Natural history museums also offer a variety of workshops, from birding to making dioramas to courses on invertebrate anatomy. At some museums, such as the American Museum of Natural History in New York, scholarships are offered.

### Clubs

Write to the National Audubon Society (see bibliography) or your local university extension service if you need help forming a nature club. Audubon Clubs are run through grade schools. 4-H has been extending its services in all major cities, and offer programs that train parents to run local groups. They not only provide tools for urban gardening, as well as fishing rods and reels for sport fishing; they will teach leaders how to organize community service projects, such as tree planting and block sweeps. They'll even help parents write grants to raise money from local city agencies or businesses. Occasionally, they'll set up your child in an existing club, but generally they prefer you to provide the children. 4-H has helped form groups in middle-class neighborhoods, in city shelters—anywhere there are kids.

### FAMILY VISITS

Here are some ways to have a relatively unrushed, quiet experience with your kids at your city's natural resources.

1. Visit during the fall or winter. Botanical gardens are still beautiful and well patroled; the conservatories are exotic and fragrant; the zoos are less crowded.
2. Have a focus before you go. Look at a book or map of the place, prepare a little, and then go for a short period of time. But go often.
3. Bring snacks to carry; if there's a checkroom, check whatever else you can.
4. Call or stop in at the education office. At the zoo, they'll tell you about recent births, feeding schedules, and any special events.
5. Ask about self-guided tours.
6. Ask your child questions, based on anything you see (even if you don't know the answers). Asking, "Why does the polar bear have pads on his feet?" or "Why do you think he's white?" can make everybody think, and it's fun to come up with theories.
7. If you can join up with another family or two (because it's the escorting and transportation that tend to be a pain in the neck), it might make it easier to schedule these events on a regular basis.

## ON CITY STREETS

If you're interested in nature right on city streets, we highly recommend two books: Helen Ross Russell's *City Critters* (Homer, New York: American Nature Study Society, 1975) and Katherine Pessino and Lois Hussey's *Collecting for the City Naturalist* (New York: Crowell Junior Books, 1975). If you read up a bit before a stroll, you'll be surprised at what you see. Here are a few facts in the meantime that may fascinate you as you stroll:

### Squirrels

Squirrels have fabulous balance. Not only can they run across a wire or down a tree head-first but they can stop on a dime. The most typical city squirrel is the gray squirrel, and half its total length is taken up by its bushy tail—which shades it from the sun, which flares out into a parachute if it falls from a tree, which can cover it and keep it warm in winter, which is an umbrella to keep away rain, and which acts as a balancer and a rudder.

Squirrels live in tree holes, but if they can't find any, then they build nests like birds. The only difference is that their nests are completely covered, so they look like giant balls.

Of course squirrels love nuts and store thousands of them every autumn, but experts have found they can't remember where they've put a nut fifteen minutes after they've hidden it. In winter, they just take whatever they find.

Dr. Kenneth Chambers of the American Museum of Natural History has spotted a new species of city squirrel—a small black version of the city gray squirrel. These squirrels are black because they have so much melanin in their skin. They'd be fun for kids to spot, he says, and they can compare them with the black panther at the zoo. The black panther, after all—you knew this, right?—is just a melanistic leopard. If you look at it closely, you can make out the spots underneath the black!

### Pigeons, Sparrows and Starlings

The city pigeon is a rock dove; originally it came from Europe, where it lived and built nests on steep cliffs. Now it builds nests on the sheer sides of office and apartment buildings.

Kids, says Dr. Chambers, may be fascinated with this piece of information: All birds have a third eyelid, but it is particularly visible in pigeons. This eyelid is a gray skin that moves across the eye, protecting the bird by pushing away specks of dirt that might get in its eye while flying. And when mother pigeons feed their young, sticking food down the babies' throats, it automatically covers the mom's eye, so the babies' mandibles won't scratch it!

And our familiar English sparrows aren't English and aren't sparrows. They're originally from Africa and they're actually weaver finches.

Sparrows are less plentiful in cities these days because there are fewer horses around. What have horses to do with sparrows? Sparrows loved to feed on the oats in horse manure.

Starlings can mimic surrounding noises, and some can actually talk. At the American Museum of Natural History in New York City, a starling named Sam says "Hi kid."

### Plants and Trees
Although there are all sorts of trees in city parks, the trees that thrive on city streets are few, no matter what part of the country that city is in. Hardy favorites include the ailanthus, which grows everywhere and is the most common; the London plane, a big shade tree that's like the American sycamore; some poplars, although in New York City, certain poplars were banned because their roots went after water so heartily that they invaded waterpipes; and the gingko tree.

### GETTING AWAY
Here are five trips out of the city that were recommended as great fun:

1. Have a blueberry pancake breakfast in the woods. Near every city are orchards where families can pick apples in

the fall, strawberries in the spring, blueberries in August. One family recommended packing your kids into the car at dawn, along with a box of pancake mix and a griddle, and driving to an orchard. As the kids pick the blueberries, the parents make a fire and then put up blueberry pancakes for a delicious outdoor breakfast right there.

2. Go to camp. Many YMCA camps stay open all year round and allow very inexpensive family overnights. They even include nature programs and will provide you with information on cross-country skiing, rock climbing, exploring, and other activities.

3. Visit a local weather station. The U.S. Weather Bureau has some 125 weather stations in the country, but there are also over nine thousand part-time cooperative stations. Most big cities are surrounded by stations to report on changing weather that might affect local aviation. Write to the Superintendent of Documents, Government Printing Office, Washington D.C. 20402 for a list of weather stations as well as a list of other publications on the weather. Beforehand, you might want to read Eric Sloane's *Weather Book,* a classic and simple introductory book on weather.

4. Take a day trip to a meadow. Wildflowers are not only beautiful, they're safe. And it's fun to identify a living object that doesn't move. Take your kids to a colorful meadow from May to October and collect a bouquet of flowers. You can bring along Peterson's *Field Guide to Wildflowers* (Boston: Houghton Mifflin, 1968) or one of the Golden Book wildflower guides if you want to identify your pickings. And be sure to bring a wide vase with some water in it and a cork that you've made holes in.

Thread the flowers through the cork and they'll live through the trip home.

5. Take a night trip anywhere. Wake your kids up in the middle of a clear night to see the stars, or go night fishing. There is something wonderful and important about getting up in the middle of the night that makes kids appreciate and remember whatever you do. And if it's summer—the shooting star season—then this nighttime wake-up call could turn into an unforgettable event for all of you. You can bring a star chart or use the local paper's guide to the visible stars of the season. The best and simplest star books are the Golden Books, for the older child (twelvish), and H. A. Rey's *The Stars: A New Way to See Them* (Boston: Houghton Mifflin, 1970).

## AT HOME

Finally, there are many basic activities you can enjoy at home —from having pets or an aquarium, planting flowers or vegetables, and collecting leaves, to reading nature books or even watching television. The Audubon Society and National Geographic Society will send you a schedule of their TV specials. (see addresses at the end of this chapter).

You can even just talk about nature—not just nature lore but also current environmental issues, both local and national. In New York City, for example, the average street tree lives only seven years because of environment factors such as pollution and because they are often abused by the local citizenry. Preserving nature in the city is difficult, and kids can feel strongly about it, if they're made aware of it. They can even call the local parks and recreation department to find out how they can help.

The education departments of local zoos or nature preserves will also talk to you about local and state environmental issues. And the National Audubon Society has a Washington hotline, which gives background information about Audubon's position on current environment bills in Washington; that number is (202) 547–9017. If you agree with them (or not), you can call or send telegrams to appropriate parties, and the hotline will provide the phone numbers and addresses. You or your children can also call your own senator directly at (202) 224–3121 for more information on any environmental bill.

> *"Parents of city kids get very upset when they rent summer houses and their kids don't leave their sides to go exploring, or say they're bored all the time. The fact is, kids need friends, and if they can't find them in the country, they're not about to go exploring. So I say pick your country neighborhood as carefully as your city one. And don't pick on your kids if they don't want to go. I love nature but you're renting a summer house for yourself."*
>
> *—Jonathan R., Queens, New York, age eighteen*

> *"Parenting is a job that's a lot like teaching. I don't mean that, as a mother, you're an educator. You are, but what I really mean is, like some teachers, you have tenure. And that's good and bad because you tend to get lazy since you know that the next day, your kids aren't going to fire you . . . if you want to be a good parent, a refreshed parent, then go the extra mile—literally. Go camping, go to the zoo, take them on a fishing trip. This is the stuff all kids, including city kids, love the most.*
>
> *—Sandy H., Washington DC, mother of two*

# HIGHER LEARNING

*T*he day after your son gets into the school of your choice, you forget the school and all you care about is, will he be happy? My advice to parents is, ask the question "Will he be happy?" the day *before* you apply to the school of your academic choice.

—Ellen P., New York City, mother of two sons

*I* was thrilled when my eldest daughter got into a prestigious academic school. But the fact was, it was too hard for her and we switched her out. I think it's important to find a good school for your child. But it's more important that you find a school where she has a good chance to succeed.

—Cara M., Chicago

## MAKING CHOICES

In selecting a middle or high school, we must remember again the basic premise of city life: We are surrounded by opportunities, and each one may have both assets and limitations. We are always identifying priorities, making choices, and then remaining flexible enough to change those choices if they turn out to be inappropriate for our children.

In selecting a school, you're trying to decide what will produce the best academic education, the best study habits, the best set of values, the best set of friends, the best self-image for your child.

And for yourself.

You're deciding what will make you and your child happiest now and also help him in the future. And that's not easy to predict.

As one mother of two grown sons commented, "I was a pretty conscientious mother, but in my experience, what turned out to be good schools for each of my boys came as a complete surprise."

## PUBLIC VERSUS PRIVATE SCHOOL

After nursery school, the first issue for many parents is whether to send their kids to a public or a private school. For many of the mothers we spoke to, this choice was difficult; and long after their kids had gone on to college, they questioned the wisdom of whatever choice they made. If you have a dependable and very high income, you may choose a private school. But if you are in that vast middle range where private school would represent some sacrifice, you often have some thinking to do. What's important to keep in mind is that no decision need be permanent. You can start off at a good neighborhood public school and switch to a fine private school for high school. You can begin by getting the basics at a strong private school and then send your kid to the best public school in your area—a special school, a magnet school, or one of the increasing number of neighborhood schools with specialties that can attract many kids. These days, there can be as much shopping for public as private institutions.

## PRIVATE SCHOOL

Private schools are not necessarily academically better than public schools. If you choose one, you are choosing its other assets:

- Small classes;
- Relaxed, unharried teachers;
- Excellent facilities;
- A concern for the "whole" child, with strong emphasis not just on basic skills but also on music, arts, crafts, and physical education, as well as emotional and personal growth, and his ability to relate to others.
- Attention to a child's need for individuality, attention, and power. Every kid tends to know every teacher; every teacher grows up with every kid. And both feel the power to influence the system, to right an injustice at the school.
- The chance for each child to become involved in every aspect of the school community, from playing on the basketball team (without having to be a great jock) to winning a part in the school play (without having to be Laurence Olivier).

A private school has other assets, too: By picking a particular school, you are choosing an approach to learning and a level of competition that you want for your child. Last but not least, you are choosing a facility where you feel your child is safe.

On the other hand, a private school is *not* the real world. It is an elite education and often not an academically superior one. It is an expensive education. And it is often an environment in which your child becomes intimately aware of every child's social and financial status. It can be an environment that makes your child want more of both.

One Manhattan mother recalls her daughter's private school experiences: The girl attended a school with the daughter of one of the largest real estate magnates in New York City, the son of one of the city's most successful restaurateurs, and the daughter of one of baseball's most famous players. When she was six and in kindergarten, she came home from her first after-school date and said, "Mom, what's a maid? What's a suite? And can we have them, too?" When she was nine, she came home and said, "We had this talk with Allison, the kid whose father owns the Las Vegas hotel. We asked her why she gets dropped off by a chauffeur every day. Why doesn't she take a bus like all the other kids? And you know what she said? She said, 'A bus? I don't want to take a bus. The best I could do maybe . . . is take a taxi.' "

On the other hand, many private schools have a commitment to social issues. Many require community service of its students or have the flexibility to bring classes to a halt when a major city or national crisis occurs so kids can discuss what is going on. If these are matters that concern you, then it's important to ask about how the school you want your child to attend participates in community affairs. It's important to ask not just about the academic philosophy of a middle school but also about its social philosophy.

## Private School Academics

Academically, every school is a little different. Although many stress strong skills these days, it's very important to visit each school and to speak to other parents. Speak to happy ones, as well as ones who've left. Ask them some of the following questions:

1. What do they think of the top administration? The headmaster sets the tone for the whole school.
2. How closely does the school keep parents informed of their children's progress? When a child had a problem, how quickly was it brought to the parents' attention?
3. Ask parents of third and fourth graders if they are satisfied with their kids' handwriting skills. Ask six-grader parents about grammar and writing skills.
4. Which are the best teachers? Why do the schools' parents like them? Sit in on the best classes and see what you think. A good class should feel good—the kids should be comfortable and enthusiastic, but under control.
5. What special courses are given at the junior high level? At what grade level are languages taught? How many languages?
6. How does the school utilize the city programs? Do the local museums, orchestras, nature facilities, and so on, run programs with that private school?
7. Finally, although this last question should be posed with some wisdom, what are the test and college results of the graduates of the school you're considering? Reading scores, SATs, and a list of colleges that the last few grad-

uating class were admitted to are available to any applying parent.

## Other Issues to Consider

1. Is it a neighborhood school? Although most private schools won't admit it, for most parents, sending a kid to a school relatively close by or with kids in the neighborhood who are also attending that school is still a plus. Schools certainly want to get kids from all over the city and will promote the advantages of city travel, but you want your seven-year-old to have friends he can see easily. If you're lucky enough to have a building filled with kids or a street swelling with them, then it may not matter where your kid goes to school. But if you don't, keep the neighborhood schools in mind, at least up until high school. As one grown-up said about social life in New York City, "It's not like the suburbs. Here it helps a lot to have a friend with the same zip code."

2. What are the mood, the philosophy, and the standards of the school? A school should have good academics, but traditional tough standards are not themselves proof of this. Speak to the Independent Admissions Association of your city for a list of your city's private schools describing their philosophies toward children. Interview top administrators at the schools. They each advertise their schools' assets in very clear ways. Said Barclay Palmer of the New York Friends' School, for example, "You have to decide just how much power and prestige you really want. Some schools have lower status. Some seem above and beyond that. The Quaker schools, i believe, are like that. If you were to ask me to succinctly state the goals we

have for our graduates, it would be 'intellectual strength and moral courage.' "

3. Who will be your children's classmates? How many are in her grade? How many boys? Girls? The advantage of a private school is its smallness. The flip side of that is that its smallness means that a child may have less of a choice of friends. Make sure there are enough kids to choose from and, preferably, a variety of types of kids. For the mothers we spoke to, the surprise element of private school often had to do with friendship and social life. The academics of middle schools were usually predictable or at least had been studied by parents in advance. But a youngster won't do well academically where he is a social misfit.

## HOW TO BE INVOLVED IN PUBLIC OR PRIVATE SCHOOL

How can you best monitor your child's education in either type of school? Actually, in both cases, your actions will be the same, but perhaps public school parenting requires you to be a little more assertive. As one public high school dean said to us, off the record, "When you take exams to get promoted in public school, there are questions about how to deal with irate parents. Generally, the right answer comes down to, 'Try to maintain the status quo—politely.' That's the way *I* answer those questions and I keep getting promoted! I can't help it. I'm so busy that, to me, parents are a pain. So I advise parents who are dealing with people like me to persist. To listen, to try to be objective about what we tell them about their child —but, if they're not satisfied, to persist. I'm only going to really act if you make me feel like a person, not a bureaucrat."

The key to surviving in the city schools, public or private, is to make the experience as personal as possible for everyone concerned. Consider the following steps to making your child's educational experience a meaningful one for both of you:

- Join the PTA.
- Go to the meetings on the class curriculum every year. Offer time, art supplies, photocopying, juice, a rug—anything. Both public and private schools often need contributions.
- Keep in touch with the administration and the teachers. Even in a public school, you can request a teacher. Write a polite letter to the principal, saying something like: "Dear Mrs. Johnson, My son Jonathan has an active, inquisitive learning style, and I feel she would thrive with so-and-so, who has a teaching style that complements those attributes. I think they would be a good match." You might even send notes to the teacher at times when you think the kids are getting too much homework or at times when they get assignments they love. You might even send a thank-you note at the end of the year. Remember, as a parent, you are an employer. You have the ability to bring out the best in any teacher.
- Monitor your child's homework. Check the amount, the difficulty, and how your child handles it. (You can point out mistakes, but don't do it for him, no matter how tempting. And if you can't resist the temptation, stay away.)
- Go to teacher conferences. Even if the teacher has

150 kids, conferences will help you get the teacher to know *your* child. Describe your kid. Make sure the teacher knows your child's record and background—academically, emotionally, physically, and so on.
- Finally, remember what Dr. David Kelley, a psychologist and consultant to several private schools in New York, says: "No matter how your kid is doing, always remember to be on his side. If he comes home and has failed a course, you don't want to say, 'How could you do this?' but, 'How can I help?'" That strikes us as good advice.

## PUBLIC SCHOOL

Every city's school situation is different, but the general assets of a public school are:

- It's free;
- It is based on the American premise of an equal education for all and is therefore what most of us were brought up to believe in. We don't feel like hypocrites when our kids go to public schools;
- Many public school parents tell us that public school kids seem to care less about material wealth or social status. Public schools rarely promote a feeling of being deprived in a middle-class child. If anything, these children feel conscious of being a *have* in a *have-not* world.
- Public schools have skilled professional staffs, often with more graduate education and a tougher approach to learning than many private schools. This is particularly true of older teachers. In both public and private schools, the quality of younger teachers depends on starting salaries. If

209

the starting salary is high, they will continue to attract good teachers.

If you are lucky enough to be in an area with a good public school, can travel to a magnet school, or are admitted to a specialty public school, there still may be drawbacks to any public school.

The public school is a tougher environment to endure in what is already a pretty tough city for a kid. In public school most kids are on their own. If one or two teachers know your kid well, you're lucky.

And most parents have little power to change things unless they spend time in parent organizations. In a big school, the average child is not going to be in the school play, on the school basketball team, or part of the school paper. Each of these becomes not an activity but an achievement, a credit toward college that only the elite of public school can enjoy.

When choosing a public school, ask the administrations, other parents, and kids these questions:

1. Is there an active parent organization and what does it do? Does it raise money for extra programs? Monitor social problems? Help foster a family spirit among teachers, kids, and parents? An active parent organization is key to maintaining some private control in a public school.
2. Is the school safe? City schools are mixed schools. That is their asset. But how do they handle either difficult kids or neighborhood problems? What is the mood of the hallways? Can kids walk to class alone? Can they feel comfortable in the lunchroom? What is the outside security like in keeping out strangers? What is the inside security?

Have there been any incidents at the school, and if so, what actions were taken to prevent future incidents? Talk to kids. Find out what their experience has been.

3. What are the class size and the mood in the classrooms? Visit some classes. Are the teachers happy and conveying enthusiasm to the students? Or does the faculty seem overworked? How much time is spent, as they say in education, "on task,"—that is, teaching, as opposed to disciplining, covering school business, et cetera.

4. What are the reading levels and test scores of kids attending the school? And why are they high or low?

5. At the higher grade levels, from fourth grade up, what special schools are available? Or what regular schools, including junior high and high schools, have been funded for special programs? Rochester, New York, a typical small city, already has magnet schools specializing in computers, business, science, humanities, and cooking. New York City has a school fair every year in which all public schools participate and advertise their educational wares.

One New York City mother sent her son David to a small private school until eighth grade. He is now attending an excellent academic public high school. "David happens to love public school," she says. "He spends many happy mornings on the bus, playing poker. He spends many happy afternoons in the back of his math class, playing poker." In public school, she says, most kids learn the system, learn how to survive— and get a kick of it.

This mother remembers fondly that at David's private school, he came home as a small boy bursting with knowledge, with questions, with a sense of wonder. And now, she says with equal but different enthusiasm, he comes home bursting with savvy.

We don't know if there's always one answer to the public versus private school question. Certainly, if you believe in either public school or private school *über alles*, then your choice is simple. But if you're one of the many parents who is uncertain, it will depend on your values, your city, each school, and, most of all, on your child. What seems ideal is finding a school where your child will receive the best city education possible — where there's always a sense of wonder — and of reality. If you find such a school and it's private, so be it. And if it's public, all the better.

# CITY MINDS, CITY VALUES

*I*t is possible to give a child a happy childhood, where he can have good feelings about himself and the world, and a zest for living. It can be done in New York, in Oshkosh, in Anchorage. It does not matter where.

—Dr. William H. Koch, child psychiatrist

*W*e need to get educated about being parents. We need to learn what's appropriate for a child. We need to get to know our children.

—Dr. Sandra Rodman Mann, mother,
family therapist, and assistant professor
of parent education, Fordham University

From the moment you bring your city baby home from the hospital, you are exposing your child to the particular pressures of city living. His responses to city stresses will depend to a large degree on the temperament he was born with; and if you watch him carefully, you will begin to see which ones bother him the most. When your child is still a baby, you can easily protect him from the stressful elements of the city. But as he grows and needs and wants independence from you, your opportunities to shield him from city pressures become scarcer. And as your child becomes a member of an academic community and a social community of his own, the stresses he encounters will increase. When he travels around his city unaccompanied by you, he will be exposed to the same trials you often are: crime, crowding on public transportation, strangers on the street. Does an urban environment have a negative effect on our children? Or, as one father bluntly asked, "Is a city childhood going to turn my kid into a nut?"

We couldn't find a single study about the effects of city living on middle-class children, which is an interesting fact in itself. "It has never been established that city pressures—noise, crowding, pollution—have a negative impact on mental health," says Dr. Norman Sussman, associate professor of psychiatry at New York University School of Medicine. "We all —adults and kids—filter out elements, like excessive noise, that we can't handle. Children," he says, "in any case, are more influenced by their parents and their peers than by any other aspect of their environment."

Dr. William H. Koch, a child psychiatrist and the founder and director of the Skhool for Parents at Lenox Hill Hospital in New York City, agrees: "The child's most important universe is the home," he says. "If the home is one where the child gets encouragement, support, and direction from his parents, outside influences are less important."

Nevertheless, a city environment can make it difficult to raise a child. We are routinely confronted with situations that test our values, with rampant consumerism, with the fast pace and lack of time that often characterize city life. "Yes, there are particular problems for city children," says Dr. Koch, "and they can be compensated for. But a parent has to recognize them and deal with them." The city parent, especially, needs skill, strategy, and thoughtfulness.

We heard again and again from child development experts that the one thing that will ensure your child's ability to deal with the stresses of city living and with stresses endemic to growing up is a strong, trusting relationship with his parents. "There simply is no stronger influence on a child than his parents," says Dr. Mann. "And when you know your child, you can help him develop coping skills that will enable him to function well independently from you." Knowing your child and being aware of pitfalls can reduce the amount of stress your child is exposed to.

## TIME WITH YOUR CHILD

Staying close to our kids may be more difficult when we're leading hectic lives; our kids wind up spending more time alone or unsupervised with peers or watching television. When kids do spend too much time alone, they feel lonely and frustrated and, as they grow, may seek to allay those feelings in inappropriate ways. If a child spends too much time unsupervised with his peers, then peer pressure, says Dr. Mann, may override his inclination to have a mind of his own; if he spends too much time watching television, he is going to be exposed to issues beyond his understanding with no one to interpret them for him.

"How do children lose their childhoods?" asks Dr. Koch.

City kids ask more questions and learn more because of what they see out on the streets. These kids are watching a Thanksgiving Day parade. (PHOTO BY BRENT PETERSEN)

"They lose their childhoods watching television." Though excessive television viewing among children is not specifically a city problem, the lack of time many city parents have for their kids and the space restrictions common in cities can exacerbate the problem. "There's a tendency for the TV to become the backyard when a family lives in a small city space," says a mental health counselor at New York City's Hudson Guild. "Instead of saying, 'Go outside and play,' parents begin to find it acceptable to say, 'Let's get a video, or see what's on TV.' "

Still, taking time out to be with our children is crucial, if often difficult. "Spending 'quality time' with your children can become a tyranny just like anything else," says Alan R. Gordon of the Stress Workshop in New York City. "What you and your kids need together is time when there's no battle of the wills going on—a calm, affectionate time." From the busy parent's point of view, setting up this kind of time may require a lot of organizing. "Among city parents," Gordon says, "overscheduling is a big problem. I suggest to people with overscheduling problems that they write down everything they do on a daily basis; I have them put together a hierarchy of goals. Then I have them do the same with roles. They have to ask themselves things like, 'How much time do I spend as a daughter? Can I cut down on phone time with my friends or with business associates at home?' "

"When things get really hectic at the office," a lawyer mother told us, "and I have to stay late, and I'm not seeing my son nearly as much as I need to or he needs me to, my first inclination is to start bringing things home for him. A toy one night, a book another. I'm so rushed during those times I don't even get to give them to him. The housekeeper does. I know it's not right, but I'm trying to keep connected with my son. One day I asked him if he liked something I had bought for

217

him and he told me, 'You didn't give me that, Mom, Elena did.' I was heartbroken, but I learned something. Nothing substitutes for the connection."

A parent suffering from guilt at leaving a child often feels that the way to reengage her is through activity. The parent may plan lots of things to do with the child, instead of focusing on her, says Dr. Mann, or has a babysitter take the child around to more activities than the child wants, needs, or can handle, instead of spending relaxed time with her. "It's hard to make the transition back to my kids after I've been spending a couple of weeks late at the office," says another harried parent. "I want to know everything my sons are thinking; everything they've been doing for the past two weeks. It puts tremendous pressure on them. One night my younger son was setting up a little train set; he knew what he was doing, but I wanted to be involved with him. So I was hanging around, giving him encouragement, and he says to me, 'Dad, could you sit down or watch TV or something? You're making me really nervous.' My kids are at a different pace than I am; it takes me a while to start to feel comfortable with them again."

## ISOLATION

Another particular urban stress, according to Dr. Koch, is caused by isolation from an extended family, especially from the child's perspective. As we all know well, urban parents often lack the natural network of neighbors and family our suburban counterparts benefit from. Working parents, especially, spend most of their time in an environment not conducive to the discussion of child-rearing concepts: In an office, it can be hard to find a sympathetic person to talk to about your terrifying discovery, only minutes ago, that your child is the only one not toilet trained in his nursery school class. "The panic I felt during the months after I went back to work was unbelievable," one mother told us. "No one in my office had young children, and Bonnie was my first. When some mother I'd never seen before would tell me on a Saturday in the park that her baby was doing this or doing that, I'd be making an instant comparison with my daughter. If I'd been talking with lots of other mothers whose kids were all different, like they all are, it would have been so much easier for me. I did finally develop a network of mother friends by getting in touch with the women who were in my Lamaze class and with women from the park, but it took a long time, and it took work."

If a network of parent friends is important to the city parent, it is equally important to the city child. The school-age city child needs the companionship of adults other than his parents, adults he can trust and can turn to when he feels angry at his parents and needs the guidance and the advice of another adult. There are two things city parents can do to ameliorate the problem of isolation, says Dr. Koch. The first is to encourage your child to express his feelings, particularly his angry feelings to you. Dr. Koch insists that if you establish good communication patterns with your child, he really won't want to keep much from you, even as an adolescent. The second is deliberately to build a network of other parents that you and your child can rely on to share feelings with.

## GETTING AROUND

*"I can't imagine my son—he's three and a half—ever, I mean ever, taking a subway by himself. Taking a subway to school every day? Never. We're going to be moving out of the city."*
—Marion C., New York City

One of the urban stresses that seems to hit city kids and city parents hardest is simply getting around town. Actually, it's not simple at all, and that's why getting around most cities is a loaded issue for parents and kids. "My daughters are both fearful," a Chicago mother told us. "I've raised them to be fearful. I want them to be aware that, as young women, they will be potential targets. I've felt that one of my choices in raising them has been that I could teach them not to be overly careful about their safety, or else to be real aware. I've taught them to be real aware. I'd rather they were overcautious than not cautious enough."

Since parents need to be more protective of their kids in cities, says Dr. Koch, children are more likely to be infantilized. A city parent, then, has a more difficult time fostering independence in her child. One thing that would greatly help, says environmental psychologist Roger Hart, would be a pocket guide to public transportation for the children of our cities, with special notations about where they can find a safe haven in a particular area and with notations about how to get to places they can enjoy on their own. In those cities where most of the population doesn't own cars, kids, out of necessity, learn how to get around town earlier than their suburban counterparts and benefit from the freedom mobility offers them. City parents are often proud of the way their kids have mastered the public transportation system: "I haven't taken a bus in fifteen years," one St. Paul mother told us, "but my daughter knows the bus system inside out. She's extremely self-sufficient in that respect, and it's given us both freedom that, in the city, we really need."

"Look, it's like everything else in the city," said another mother. "The more you use public transportation, the smarter about it you are. You know what looks weird and what doesn't. That's the way my son learned about getting around town. First with me—he's been taking buses and trains all his life—and then on his own. I know he knows how to handle himself, because time and again I've seen him do it."

One of the stressful things about public transportation in any city—though the problem varies from city to city—is that you're at the mercy of a system that frequently works poorly and is subject to the congestion of city traffic. Even when you're very deliberate about leaving yourself plenty of time to get somewhere, there's a good chance you're going to be late. "I chose my lifelong motto very carefully," said one mother. "And I very carefully passed it on to my children. I got it from Mel Brooks's two-thousand-year-old man: Never run for a bus, he said. There'll always be another."

## SOCIAL AND ACADEMIC COMPETITION

*"This is the limit, I said to myself: Someone told me that the nursery school I was thinking about sending my son to was giving intelligence tests to the parents."*
—*Marilou M., New York City*

We found even the most unflappable parents have the tendency to start flapping when they have to start thinking about getting their kids into school. Mothers of very young children —ages two to four—told us they sent their kids to nursery school mostly because of peer pressure. "I took my daughter out of nursery school for the day," said one mother. "We went to the playground. There was no one there her age. If I didn't send her to school, she'd have no one to play with." The stress

221

about sending your child to school starts very early in parent-hood. And that's just the beginning.

Once kids begin school, it can be a major issue for parents to deal with their own competitive feelings and their children's.

But it is almost always parental stress, says Dr. Mann, that ultimately affects the child. "Most academic problems are with the parents, not the children," she says. "If both parents are working or both feel guilty about not spending enough time with the child, they are more likely to feel that they have to show that their kids are more proficient or that they're doing well. So it's more important to those parents that their children get into the 'right' school and excel in that school. And so they come down harder on the children."

If it's extremely important to you that your child get into a particular school, it's a good idea to examine your motives. Do you have more invested in it than that he get a good education? Is there nowhere else in your city that he can get a good education?

Alan R. Gordon of the Stress Workshop in New York City suggests that, to make it easier on your child, you should apply to one school you know he will get into and another you really want him to get into—and then push them both equally to the child. Another successful approach for some parents has been to be completely candid with their child: "I told my son, 'You can be happy in *this* school, and you can be happy in *this* one. It'll be very flattering if you're accepted in the first school, but you will also get a good education and meet wonderful people in the second.'" But you have to acknowledge your child's inevitable disappointment if he doesn't get into the school he and his friends most want to go to, and help him deal with it.

If your child feels there's only one school worth getting into, and he's rejected, he's likely to feel that the school he winds up at is second rate and therefore that he is second-rate, too, notes Dr. Koch. "These kids don't feel good enough about themselves," he says. "They get turned off by school. They don't feel loved for themselves."

No matter what his grade standing, it's important to recognize and appreciate your child's capabilities, says Dr. Mann. If your child is enrolled in an academic community where all the kids are pretty bright in the first place, it's sometimes hard to do that. But finding the areas your child is good in, is crucial. When the competition is tough, that's where your child's self-esteem will come from. "The standard for achievement in the school my daughters are in is extremely high," one mother told us. "In another school, they would be at the very tops of their classes, but in the school they're in, they're only middle-of-the-class students. So there is not often a lot of self-esteem where there should be. You know, when I told my younger child how well she reads, she said, 'But look how well my friend Natasha reads; I'm not really very good at all.' That hurts me. So I tell my daughter how wonderful she is, all the time. I tell her that people are good at different things. I make sure—and this is very important—that my girls have the chance to develop the skills they excel at. One is a great swimmer, so I've made sure that she's always been in a swimming club."

Social pressures, too, often stem from the parents, says Dr. Mann. "In most cities," she points out, "the pace is faster, the opportunities are greater, the pressures to do more are intensified. Often parents get involved in competing with their neighbors and wind up exposing their kids to too much too soon." Parents' expectations then become inappropriate, she says, and they get panicky when they see one child doing something if their child isn't doing it, too. It's easy in the city

223

for parents to lose their perspective on things; they get their kids involved in a lot of after-school activities because it's convenient, or they throw birthday parties that are too extravagant. The final result of this kind of competition is that the child feels stressed.

"One of the ways your child learns to please you is by recognizing what your expectations are for him and then trying to fulfill them," says Dr. Mann. "When parents are overwhelmed by competition with other families, the child will feel that. The child will feel that he must have the best birthday party or the best apartment or the best clothes. It puts tremendous pressure on kids. These kids are often more fashionable at a younger age, use more sexual and social posturing, are more tense and tough. It's sad," Dr. Mann continues, "because it all reveals an underlying anxiety that they won't measure up, and it comes from their home system."

"It's absolutely true that parents can instill competition in their children," says Dr. Koch. "But if you communicate to your children that your values allow you to judge a person by other things than how much money he makes or what kinds of material things he owns, your child will embrace those values, too."

---

### STRESS RELIEVERS FOR CITY KIDS

- Noncompetitive or competitive sports, depending on what your child most enjoys;
- Time spent doodling on musical instruments (or formal training, but *only* if your child is interested);
- Time with surrogate parents whom your kids can confide in and who won't put pressure on them;
- Taking his own time; the best thing you can do to

prevent your child from being stressed is not to accelerate him;
- Plenty of time for physical activity in a park or a gym;
- Escaping from the city for a few hours, for a day, for a weekend;
- Socializing as a family with other families;
- Free time alone, without playdates, and also unstructured play-date time;
- Unplanned time with parents;
- Reading with parents, right through their adolescence.

## SOCIAL PRECOCITY, SEXUAL PRECOCITY, AND VALUES

One of the most prevalent fears city parents have is that a life in the city is somehow robbing their kids of a "real" childhood. One father told us, "On the first warm evening, I start thinking about how my friends and I used to meet after dinner and hang out till dusk when the streetlights came on. My son can't go out after dinner unless I go with him; and even then, it's too late to go to the park. It saddens me. I'm not talking on a Huck Finn scale, you know."

But the delights of childhood have little to do with innocence. It is not the city that influences how fast our children grow up, but more universal things, such as television and the amount of time and the kind of time we spend with our kids.

Marie Winn, author of *Children Without Childhood* (New York: Penguin, 1984) wrote that she was surprised to find that precocity was not an urban phenomenon, and that children's precocity related instead to whether parents were divorced and whether both worked outside the home. "It . . . became apparent to me that the great social changes that have set in during the last two decades have been far more influential in changing

225

relations between adults and children and defining children's position in society than any possible regional difference," she writes. But if the city does have a fast track for children, how does a parent prevent a child from being sucked onto it?

Dr. Mann believes that a city gives a parent great opportunities to pass along values and to shape a child's life: "There are more moments when a parent and a child share important things in a city," she says. "City kids ask more questions, because they see more. The more questions your child asks, the more involved you will be in influencing him. I call it incidental learning."

"When my son first noticed pornography," she says, "I asked him, 'How does that look to you?' My first intent was to let him know that I knew he was seeing it and that it didn't have to be a secret. Then, because I think it's important to understand why women get involved in pornography, we talked about why some women do; and after that I tried to give him a slow, careful introduction to what I think about it."

## RACISM

When we brought up the issue of racism in our cities, this is what we heard: If you really want to see racism, get out of the cities and into the suburbs and small towns. Middle-class city parents and kids most often told us that racism didn't seem to be a problem for them. After having been raised among people of many different races, they felt they truly believed that all people are created equal.

In other words, the parents and kids we spoke to were overall quite sophisticated about racial prejudices—which can be good and can be misleading.

The more sophisticated we are about our prejudices, the better we are at hiding them, from each other and from ourselves. It wasn't easy to get a New York mother to admit: "There's one reason for the residue of prejudice among people like me who should know better. It seems more likely that if anyone's going to perpetrate violence on me, it's going to be a Black or a Hispanic. I don't even know if that's statistically true, but that's the way it feels." The fact is, it can be a terrible struggle to keep feelings of racial prejudice in check when you are attacked or your child is. You may find yourself generalizing about a group of people because of your fear.

"But the more deeply you and your child are integrated into a multiethnic society, the less likely you'll be to draw generalizations about people under any circumstances," says Dr. Philip Spivey, a psychologist at Long Island College Hospital in Brooklyn, New York. "The portrayal of Blacks and other minorities on television news is horrendous," he continues. "So if your kid is learning mainly from TV about what minorities are like, he's going to get a pretty distorted picture. That's why it's crucial to have other multiethnic resources around. If your kid is learning from real-life experiences, the way a child can learn in the rich, diverse environment of a city, his view will be more well rounded, even if he has had a bad experience."

Dr. Spivey insists that it's critical for a parent to ask him or herself, "What do I do to increase tolerance for other kinds of people in my own life? How many of my own friends are Black, Hispanic, Mexican, Asian?" It's one thing to profess your beliefs, he says, but integrating different kinds of people into your life is what makes a difference to your child. "Your kids will incorporate humanistic values, but they must feel that your values are unqualified; you must live them so that your children can see that you do," he says.

Dr. Michael Schulman, psychologist and coauthor of *Bringing Up a Moral Child* (Reading, Mass.: Addison-Wesley, 1985), adds, "Point out similarities between people of other races and yourselves; that will help your child see people as individuals and broaden his concept of his 'family.' Point out that in the worst ghetto with the highest crime rate, the majority of the people who live there are like him and like you, and that the people who get noticed are those who cause trouble.

"You can teach your child to appreciate things about other cultures," he continues, "about different foods, music, myths. Focus on the positive, but don't gloss over the things you don't like. You can pass on to your daughter your enthusiasm for Latin music, for example, and still discuss why Latin attitudes about women bother you."

Dr. Spivey agrees: Positive attitudes about people and cultures that are different from your own lessen racist attitudes.

"I sent my kids to public schools," says one mother of four. "That way, I was sure that they were going to be exposed to the variety of races that made up our neighborhood. I'll tell you one thing: It wasn't easy for them. Our public school was very well integrated. White kids were in the minority. But my kids all learned how to cope. They found resources within their own community. What kinds of resources?" This mother laughs. "One of my kids became very tight friends with the biggest Hispanic kid in his class. And all my kids developed a great tolerance for ideas unlike their own."

It's important, experts and parents agreed, to send your child to a school with an integrated student body and faculty and with a curriculum that incorporates the history of racism in this country as well as the effects of racism today.

A Black mother whose son attends an almost all-white private school pointed out: "Even though my son goes to private school, I know the kids in public school are going to be his peers, out in the real world, when he graduates. So what's happening in the public school system is important to my child even though he's in private school now."

"We all need to pressure legislators and to work with community groups to improve the public school system," Dr. Spivey says. "It's a part of our community."

Are we contributing to racism when we don't support the public school system? "It's an old quote, but it's true," says Dr. Spivey. "If you're not part of the solution, you're part of the problem. Unless you're doing something to improve the lives of all of the children of your city, you're helping things stay just the way they are."

According to Judith D. R. Porter, author of *Black Child, White Child: The Development of Racial Attitudes* (Boston: Harvard University Press, 1971): "The racial attitudes of children are a reflection of the racial attitudes and actions of American society. Only if energy is redirected toward the improvement of the economic position of blacks and the full integration of American society will the pattern of prejudice among whites and self-rejection among black youngsters . . . disappear."

## THE POOR AND THE HOMELESS

In some cities, the problems of poverty and homelessness are so acute that we come face-to-face with them every day. Sometimes the very first questions our children ask are about the poverty they see. "When my son was two, he asked me why an old man was sleeping on the sidewalk near our doorway," a New York mother told us. "I was so surprised that he asked me about it, I wasn't sure what to say." In replying, it's important to remember what stage of development your child is going through. For example, if you tell your two-year-old that someone sleeps on the street because he has no home, your child might get the idea—ridiculous to you, but real to him if he's at a stage when he's struggling with the issues of separation and abandonment—that *he* might have to sleep on the street.

"My first instinct as a parent was to pull my kids away from anyone who looked homeless or abject," said one mother. "I felt very conflicted about it. I felt as if I were giving my kids double messages: I had this primitive urge to protect my kids, which I felt was going to instill in them the idea that these people were harmful in some way; and, on the other hand, I'd be telling them out of the corner of my mouth as I dragged them away, 'These people are victims, not criminals, they're people like us, but they have no homes and they're very poor.' "

"Every day when we walked down a couple of blocks of Broadway," said a New York mother, "my son and I would see people begging for food or money. My son's a big kid—he always wanted a slice or a snack when he got out of school for the day—and so we would buy something and he'd eat it while we were walking home. And one day, he said, 'Mom, I don't want to eat anymore in front of these people. I can't afford to give them all something, so I'd rather wait till we get home.' I felt he was being respectful; I was moved."

## DEVELOPING A SOCIAL CONSCIENCE

If it's important to you not to be passive, if community work is a part of your agenda, then it's more likely to be important to your child as well. Your child will probably do as you do, says Beth Gorrie of the Coalition for the Homeless in New York. "I would involve my child in any volunteer work I do, if it seems appropriate," she says. "Let the child see my enjoyment and satisfaction. Let the child experience it for himself."

When your child is old enough to understand the issues, you can talk about why some people don't have a place to live.

"The problem of the homeless is a housing question," says Gorrie. "I'd want a child to know that I feel angry that our government has not helped people get housing they can afford. I'd be sure my child saw that I cared about the problem and that, by calling attention to it and insisting that some kind of housing be provided for homeless people, I can help to begin to solve the problem."

Gorrie stresses that it's important not to instill an "us/them" orientation in your child and to help your child understand that it's not fair to blame the victims. It's important, she says, that your child understand that many homeless families are families like his own, but who have run into terrible circumstances.

"Intellectually, I know I should help my kids understand that some of the homeless are people like us," says one mother. "But what does that mean, 'people like us'? Yes, they're like us, except that they're hungry, and they have no home, and many of the children are abused, and they're frightened and angry. You know, I think that's a lot for a kid, even an adolescent, to deal with. It's more feasible for me to tell my kids what the specifics of their lives might be, that they may have been burned out of their homes, why the children have to be playing in an empty lot. For me it gets clearer then what we can do to help them: where can we lobby to get housing; who can we petition to have the lot cleaned out and paved, at least, if we can't have a playground. The problems still sound serious, but at least they begin to seem soluble."

Both experts and parents agree about how to encourage community involvement and to plant the seeds of a social conscience in your child: Let the child see your own involvement and *talk to him* about what you think about social issues. "Sure, I talk to my kids about social responsibility," says one mother. "But what impresses them is that they're always seeing me do things. I work in a social service agency; they see me rushing out of the house in the morning, excited about work."

Several parents we spoke to told us they encouraged their kids to take some formal religious training: "I enrolled my daughter in a communicants class to try to get her familiar with Biblical values," said one mother. "I felt religious training was one way to give my child a well-defined structure to grow up in, someplace where she could learn about the concept of equity. I don't expect her to adopt all the values, but at least she will have been exposed to them."

You can also choose a school for your child that stresses the importance of community involvement, or encourage your child's school to include that in the curriculum.

## THE MYTH OF THE PERFECT CHILDHOOD

Our city kids are exposed to a lot, and they ask a lot of questions. We want to be able to have some influence on their thinking, and so we feel that we should always be coming up with answers. We may often feel as if we're constantly evaluating our beliefs. But the point is that sharing our ideas with our kids, even when we don't have answers—and maybe especially when we don't—is one of the ways we can maintain a connection with them.

As Dr. Norman Sussman, associate professor of psychiatry at New York University School of Medicine, says, "One of the most important predictors of happy kids is happy parents." This can be very reassuring news, if you're a happy person. But if you're a—you know—basically happy person who is often beleaguered by the pressures of your career or social and family commitments, it can get you to wondering. Are there people who are happy all the time; who live balanced, stress-free lives; who feel so confident about their marriages, their child-bearing decisions, their values, that they are never concerned about whether they are setting good enough examples for their children? If there are, these people have eluded us. Or, for the sake of their image, they have lied to us. The stress-free family is a myth, just as the idea that childhood is a time of innocence and bliss is a myth.

We come to the city to experience diversity. We come because it allows for moral and emotional complexity. We want that for ourselves and for our children. So we may need to remind ourselves that we cannot give our children "perfect" childhoods. Not because of where we live, but because there is no such thing to give.

"You want to raise a child who feels good about himself, right?" says Dr. Koch. "If your child feels competent, if you've been kind and considerate to him, he will be the same to you and to other people. Your child is emulating you from the day he is born. You lead a good life, and the likelihood is that your child will, too. It doesn't matter where you do it."

# TEENS: CITY FREEDOMS AND RESPONSIBILITIES

*I* don't say you shouldn't worry about teenagers if you want to. But everyone I knew wished their parents had *more* to worry about. We didn't take drugs, we got drunk a few times, maybe; we had fun, but rarely as much as we wanted; we never had as much sex as we wanted; most of all . . . I'm still just trying to grow up. If you think you're worried . . . look a little closer at us. So are we. The nice thing about being a teenager in the city . . . was that there were always adults to look up to and talk to and learn from . . . and take our minds off ourselves with. The guys I know here from other places envy me.

—Eric B., Boston, Massachusetts, a city adolescent now in college.

*T*eenage years in the city are great. There's always something happening. The kids can be themselves, can be unconventional. The other morning my daughter's friend arrived at eight o'clock to pick her up for school in a strapless yellow evening gown and one black lace glove and three-inch heels. She was very upset because her grandmother said she looked like a whore. She did. The next day she dressed like a preppy again. But nobody stopped her. It was great.

—Janet C., New York City

Adolescence can be unpredictable. City life is even more unpredictable. But teenagers raised in the city by attentive, loving parents can be spectacular young people—at peace with themselves, enriched by and appreciative of knowledge and culture, accepting of the varieties of people and personalities, and involved and committed to their society. A city adolescent, said one enraptured parent, "is a kid who isn't embarrassed to go to museums, to show his feelings, to talk to adults. He can still 'hang out,' have fun, play ball, fall in love. But he won't feel guilty if he isn't ready or doesn't want to do the 'typical' stuff. He can find out, in a relatively accepting society, who he is."

Some city parents feel ambivalent that their younger kids didn't have a typical "Where did you go?" "Out." "What did you do? "Nothing." childhood the way they imagine suburban

236

or country children have. But most parents we spoke to were glad their kids didn't have a "typical" suburban adolescence. They wanted them to have more options, more freedom. As one Boston mother said, "Busy is beautiful. In Boston, where there is so much for them to do, so many groups to fit in to, I think kids are less likely to be bored and get into trouble. Being a teenager is hard, but being one in this city makes it a little easier."

Many veteran city parents agreed. Said one mother of a daughter just off to college, "I remember my own suburban adolescence. There weren't enough outlets for all my energy and searching. There was only one society—high school society—and if you didn't fit in, you were miserable. You had no idea that life offered other alternatives. I think my kid likes herself more than I did at her age."

A Manhattan teenager said, "Here you can experiment a little, put your toe in stuff, test the waters, and get out. I tried marijuana. I've tried drinking. I tried them and that was it." The boy's father added, "His mother and I don't worry as much, I think, here, because we knew when he did get drunk, he couldn't drive. . . . We don't need or have a car in Manhattan. Also, he can do so many adult things here. . . . I think he has less need to prove he's grown up."

These are contented city families, definitely. And, of course, such advertisements for city parenting are dangerous to generalize from. Certainly, there are great kids everywhere, there are happy kids everywhere—and troubled ones, too. An adolescent struggles to answer difficult questions about personal identity and sexual identity and independence, and these issues can create stress anywhere. The quality of family life is more important than anything else in raising happy, healthy kids. Love, attention, quantity time as well as quality time, not hurrying your kids into adulthood—all these are more important than *where* you raise your kids.

Still, we were struck by the high level of satisfaction among city parents and their teenage children, as well as by the fact that most parents felt that living in the city made being a parent of an adolescent easier.

## CITY LIMITS

Many parents stated that it was the freedom to explore, and escape convention that tempted them to a city family life. But, as a result, they said, setting limits was often harder. As one mother said, "You didn't want to set rules that you knew they wouldn't follow, but you learned soon enough—you better set limits, some limits. They need them. They *love* them."

All the experts we spoke to agreed that maintaining freedom while slowly increasing responsibility is vital to any teenager. In the city, there are the illusions that teenagers know a lot, that they can take care of themselves, that they can handle a lot of freedom—but these aren't necessarily true. One Brooklyn mother said, "Teenagers need one phrase to carry with them everywhere and we have to give it to them. And that phrase is, 'My mom won't let me.' "

City teenagers are sophisticated about city life, but it's a mistake to assume they're more sophisticated emotionally than any other adolescent. And it's particularly dangerous to assume that middle-class urban kids are more advanced socially or sexually. Family therapist Sandra Mann says, "City parents mustn't confuse sophistication—which many city kids have and which can be wonderful—with maturity. People assume that they are capable of handling sex sooner, for example. They're not. Kids develop at a certain rate emotionally and intellectually and that cannot be speeded up." Said young adult

novelist Fran Pascal, "City girls may ultimately be more sophisticated, yes, but as young teens, they're just as afraid and
scared about love, sex, and intimacy as any kid anywhere, depending on their personality and home life. They need to be
talked to, they need to be educated about sex, and they need to
know there's no need to rush into adulthood."

Another mother said, "You know, the boy on the Bill
Cosby show thinks about nothing but girls. He's my son's age
and has had four girlfriends already. My kid is sixteen, he's a
nice boy, and he just broke up with his first girlfriend. He told
his best friend (who told my best friend) that going out with
her took too much time away from handball. I mean, city or
no city, for some kids, the hormones just haven't kicked in
yet."

In other words, adolescents may have more outlets and freedom and street smarts—and temptations—in the city, but
they're confronted by many of the same problems as adolescents everywhere. There are fast-track kids, there are bored
kids, there are troubled kids; but the majority of teenagers, as
psychiatrist Daniel Offer's classic longitudinal study indicates,
do not suffer real *Sturm und Drang* for their seven adolescent
years.

---

## HELP FOR PARENTS

There are many books about adolescence, so this won't
attempt to cover all the complex issues of this period.
Some general guides that parents have recommended are:
*All Grown Up with No Place to Go: Teenagers in Crisis,* by
    David Elkind (Reading, Mass: Addison-Wesley, 1984);
*The Healthy Adolescent: A Parents' Manual,* by Barry Lau-
    ton and Arthur Freese (New York: Scribners, 1981);

*The Parents' Guide to Teenagers,* edited by Leonard Gross (New York: Macmillan, 1981);

*Understanding Early Adolescence* by John Hill (New York: Center for Early Adolescence, 1985);

And for a rather lighter approach, try *Your Adolescent: An Owner's Manual,* by Carol Eisen Rinzler (New York: Atheneum, 1981).

Some of the most popular sex education books that parents recommended to us were by Lynda Madaras. They include *The What's Happening To My Body? Book for Boys* and *What's Happening to My Body? A Growing-Up Guide for Mothers and Daughters.* Both are published by Newmarket Press, New York.

Besides books, many experts and parents recommend finding a parenting workshop in your city, a workshop that is geared to local parenting problems. An excellent source of information for such groups is either the local university's child development center; the nearest school of social work; or the Family Resource Coalition, a national federation of more than two thousand organizations dedicated to developing prevention-oriented, community-based programs to strengthen families and help parents. Write to the Family Resource Coalition, 230 North Michigan Avenue, Suite 1625, Chicago, Illinois 60601, for a monthly updated list of parenting groups. This group can not only provide information and resources on support groups but will direct you to help on particular issues, such as drug or alcohol abuse, single parenting, sex education, and prevention of child abuse.

There are temptations in the city, however. In cities with good public transportation, city adolescents can be more independent. They need specific rules. Here are several essential ones that psychologists and city parents have urged us to recommend:

- *Set a curfew,* no matter how much your kid complains. While a teenager is living with you, even until the age of nineteen or twenty, there should be a specified time by which she must be home. The average thirteen- to fifteen-year-old should be home by dinnertime on weeknights, with perhaps a ten o'clock midweek curfew one night a week. Midnight is late enough for weekends. For fifteen- to seventeen-year-olds, a two A.M. weekend curfew is late enough, and even that should be restricted to *one* weekend night a week.

  In smaller communities, where parents know one another and can agree on general guidelines, setting curfews might be easier. But in cities, where kids often change schools, private high schools encourage parents to organize and set such rules. In big public schools, where parents begin to lose touch with other parents, many feel alone and unsupported ("Ma, nobody else has to be home by two in the morning! You are so out of it!") Get a class list at your child's school, get names of friends whom they party with, and talk to other parents. One mother said, "When my son was fifteen, one of his friend's mothers called me—a complete stranger. She just wanted to know if my son was going to the same party her son was going to and if I'd set a curfew. We set one together on the phone. I was so glad she called."

- *Know where your children are.* Make them tell you where they're going and when. And if they're going to be late or

241

if they're going from one location to another, then they *must* call and let you know.

One parent said, "I guess I'd call myself permissive. I don't have a lot of rules. But my kids think I'm strict, because I say the rules like I'm King Henry VIII. That seems to make a difference. One night, I heard my son Josh saying to friends, 'My father goes crazy, really crazy if I break curfew. He's a madman. What can I do? He's a worrier.' He said 'He's a worrier' like 'He's a bleeder.' But I'm telling you, he said it with pride."

• *Insist that any parties your adolescent attends are chaperoned.* This, admittedly, is not an easy rule to enforce. Every psychologist we spoke to with preadolescent children delivered this rule as hard and fast. City parents and psychologists with teenage children tempered it with some qualifications, as follows:

If the party is at your house and you don't want to be in the way (especially if your apartment is small), go out and come back at the crucial hour, around eleven P.M. when trouble is likely to start. Be a little overprotective. Check the kids' condition and transportation home, drive them home, or put them in cabs.

If the party is at another parent's house, call and ask the parents if and when they'll be present, what restrictions there are, and so on. Says Marie Winn, mother of two grown sons and author of *Children Without Childhood*, "I always called. My sons pretended to hate it...but I think they were glad I did. And I said to them, 'It's my problem. I worry and I need to do this.'"

On the other hand, there is a new kind of city party at which the chaperone rule is proving tough to enforce. Five or six high school students rent a hall and other kids pay $5 admission to cover the costs. There may be beer there

or, often, marijuana. These parties are a fad, and it is difficult to forbid your kids to go to them. A fifteen-year-old girl
told us, "I go. I stay out of the drug area. I have a beer so I
don't seem like a nerd, and I have fun. Most kids I know
can handle it. Some can't... but their parents don't seem
to care." Said Francine Pascal, who is the mother of three
grown city girls, "Look at each kid. Be attentive. If you pay
attention, you can tell if your child is in trouble, is on drugs,
is prone to trouble. If the day after one of these parties,
you observe them closely and they seem fine, they probably are. I think, in that case, it's important to let yourself go
with the odds. But I also think that you have to be prepared to be honest with yourself. Sometimes parents don't
want to face the fact that a kid is in trouble."

If you have doubts about the safety of your child or any
child you care about, there is one other thing you can do.
Find out where these parties are held and who rented the
space. The renter is legally liable if liquor or drugs are
served.

In some cities, social life begins at eleven o'clock at
night. Clubs open, the streets become active, and so do
the teenagers. Again, it's difficult to forbid your child to
stay home when his or her peers are all out there. But if
you honestly think your child can't handle it or that you'll
worry, forbid it!

Set up strict rules about drugs or alcohol, as well as
guidelines for love and sexual relationships that you believe in. Enforce them as best you can.

• *Define your own values.* Parents of adolescents sometimes
have a difficult time because their own teenage struggles
with sex or drugs or values come back. And since these
values seem to change somewhat in every generation, the
ideals or life-style you believed in when your child was a

toddler may not be standards you're so sure of now. Child-rearing rules and sexual mores don't stand still—and where you may have felt permissive ten years ago, now you may feel that your children's sexual lives should be controlled—that they should be virgins or love people before sleeping with them; that they should be careful about diseases; and that they *should, should, should.* It's hard when, for the first ten years of their life, you may have believed they *could, could, could.*

Says Dr. Mann, "The values you raised your kid with for the first thirteen years are the values your child will ultimately test in adolescence." Think about your own life—deep down, no matter how different you are from your parents, your values about how to relate to people are probably remarkably similar. If you've taught your child to respect people, if you treat your mate with respect, if you are demonstrative, your child will be too."

- *Pay close attention to your kids' friends and their relationships with them.* Be there to talk when there's trouble with these relationships.

One of the great things about cities is that there are many groups and crowds, for teens as well as children. But they are, said one parent, "often in flux. Best friends move. Change schools. Spend weekends with a newly divorced father in the country. Or even break up with each other. It's hard to keep track."

But it's vital to keep track. On the one hand, more options for friends and groups can be wonderful for teenagers. Said one mother, "My daughter is a difficult kid. She didn't get along with kids from Day One. At fourteen, we sent her to a family therapist. Then, at the counselor's suggestion, we looked for a group of new kids where she could start over. We're not religious, but we found a friend whose kid went to a temple youth group. She invited Jennifer, who is now totally involved in a weekly 'rap' group there. They talk, have parties, socialize, but it's incredibly straight and middle class and supervised—and she loves it. It took time, and I'm not saying there are no problems, but we found the right group for her."

Helping a child change schools, friends, and hobbies can be very valuable when a teenager goes through a difficult period, and it's easier to make these changes in a city. Said Sandra Mann, "If having and taking options is a sign of mental health, then city kids may well have a better chance at being healthy."

On the other hand, all these options must be monitored. Get to know your teenager's friends. Ask their names, ask about their families, be a pain in the neck. Encourage your kids to have their friends up to your house at a time when you can meet them. Often, if you sit around with kids and listen, they love it. They'll bend your ear (if you don't bend theirs). You'll learn something. It takes time, but it's well worth it.

- *Establish a reasonable amount of time every week when you and your teenager are home together.* There's more to do in cities, for both kids and parents, and since sometimes there's family tension, it's often easier to stay apart. But it isn't wise. One mother said, "We really needed that rule. I could work sixty hours a week if my boss demanded it, and Stephen could stay out with his friends seven days a week. I know peers are important to teenagers, but so is a family life; and I know he was flattered and pleased that we made a rule that my husband, two sons, and I spend at least every Sunday together. We have dinner together— as a loose rule—three nights a week. No dates are allowed, unless their friends want to join us. It's family night."

245

Enforcement, of course, is as important as setting up any of these rules in the first place. You can threaten a kid with no TV for a week, but you have to follow through. Can you trust him to obey a rule or follow a punishment such as no TV when you're not around? One mother told us, "Don't trust them. Don't tempt them. If you've forbidden TV, lock it away. Don't leave it in the house. You're expecting too much of them."

How strictly you need to enforce any rule depends on your child. Said another mother, "I have two sons. One loved the responsibility of the honor system. The other couldn't handle it. So I was stricter and left him fewer options. And when he screamed, 'You don't trust me,' I'd say, 'I love you, but I don't trust your ability to restrict your computer games.' It would have been like putting me in a room with cigarettes when I was trying to stop."

Dr. David Elkind, one of this decade's most well-known child psychologists, in his book *All Grown Up and No Place To Go: Teenagers in Crisis,* (Reading, Mass: Addison-Wesley, 1984) urges us to lay down rules even if we can't always enforce them. If we believe smoking is bad for them, we can forbid it even though we know they might smoke when they are out of our view. He suggests we tell them, "I know that you can smoke when you are elsewhere. But each time I find out about it, you will be grounded and have your allowance cut in half." "Just because we don't have total control," he writes, "doesn't mean we have no control."

Dr. Arnold Cohen, a psychiatrist specializing in adolescent development, adds, "All parents, not just fast-track parents, are tempted to spoil their kids, to give them everything, including freedom. It's hard to set limits and enforce them. But remember that adolescents need to live with a process of frustration, delay, and eventual mastery; they need 'no's for basic development. Freud suggested that aggressive and sexual drives be inhibited and believed that, when they are, they're subliminated into more productivity. Into 'better stuff.' So—forgetting morality—it makes sense in terms of helping the development of a productive human being to say no!"

One critical point about transgressions. No matter what rule an adolescent breaks, what infraction is committed, what behavior he fails at, you still want to make it clear you're on his side. "You disapprove of an *action,* but you still love *your child,"* says Dr. David Kelley, a psychologist in private practice in Manhattan. "The most important thing to do is to talk together... from childhood on... to keep talking, and to tell your children that, if they get in trouble, to come to you. That no matter what—no matter how scared they are about how you'll feel... you'll never abandon them... you'll listen.

## ACADEMIC PRESSURES—COLLEGE BOUND

It's one thing to want your kid to be happy and successful when she's young. But once high school arrives, many a parent loses perspective. The pressure on kids mounts to succeed at school and get into a good college. You can help your kids survive academic pressures and get into an appropriate school.

First of all, remember who they are. Said one young man, a sophomore at a prestigious private school, "I'm smart, but I'm not a genius. I thought my parents knew that. But, all of sudden, when I mention a friend is applying to Harvard, they look at me like I'm a big disappointment."

Remember who they are and get them help when they need it. If they fail a course, try to stay calm. Get a tutor, either through their school or by calling the appropriate department of your local university and asking for a student tutor who is majoring in that field.

Second, keep in mind that choosing a college can be overwhelming and scary for a teenager, especially in high-pressured, competitive city schools. Kids may seem not to care, but they do. They just can't act. So get involved. Said one mother, "You have two choices: screaming or doing it yourself. Ask what schools they might be interested in and send away for catalogues. Arrange college tours. But stay calm. And don't obsess!"

If you can afford it, sign up your child for an SAT prep course. The SATs are supposed to be aptitude tests, but preparation helps, and almost every parent we spoke to recommended them. There are three types of courses. The Princeton review program emphasizes tricks and weaknesses in the SATs. If you don't take the course, its book *Cracking the System* by Adam Robinson and John Katzman (New York: Villard, 1986) gives you the main ideas. The Stanley Kaplan schools emphasize building a base of knowledge and provide a great deal of study material, often more than kids have time to learn. (Kaplan, however, was unofficially recommended by a college board official we spoke to.) Finally, there are excellent smaller courses, such as the currently popular Advantage Testing in New York, which combines techniques of both. Advantage and other smaller courses limit the class size to under twelve students and provide a lot of individual attention or extra tutoring, so it can be especially helpful for kids who, as they say, "don't test well."

## FAMILY TIME

Even families who've spent lots of time together when the kids were little often talk about drifting apart during adolescence. These drifts tend to occur for many reasons. Teenagers do want and need to be independent. We can now let our kids go off for a few hours and not worry about where they are. As they start to be independent, many city parents, with lives of their own, are also eager to let them go. They crave privacy. Single parents seek the company and support of their friends, need time to date, and are often relieved to create the distance that sometimes is necessary for adult sanity, since adolescents can be so difficult. As one mother said, "One day he was talking English and the next, he was talking adolescent." Besides, said many parents, they became wary of spending too much time with their kids. Some single parents were worried about using their kids for companionship too much. Some parents worried that teenagers who wanted to hang out with their families were immature. After all, teens are not *supposed* to want to be with you anymore.

But they *do* want to be with you. They just may not want to be *seen* with you. You will inevitably embarrass them, but if you're not around, they'll miss you. A lot.

Every parent and expert we spoke to stressed how much teenagers need you to be home as much as you can be, no matter how grown up they seem. And although city kids may seem to suffer less from boredom, they, too, may be home alone too much. They, too, need company or supervision. As Cloe Madanes, codirector of the Family Therapy Institute of Washington, has said, "Teenagers need a babysitter as much as younger children do."*

Fortunately, said many parents, the potential for a balance between independence and family closeness is part of city family life. One mother of a fourteen-year-old city boy said, "Paradoxically, I think city adolescents *can* be more independent, but at the same time, they tend to be closer to you, to know you better because of smaller apartments, because the city parents I know are talkers, and because there are more events in the city that you really could enjoy together." Said another, "Just like every teenager, every family has to search for an identity, an interest they really enjoy developing together. If you do that, whether it's music or sports or card games, even —you'll be all right."

One of the best ways to be together with your children, besides being in the same house at the same time, is to continue to do kid things as well as adult things together. Movies are great, dinners are fun, but as young-adult author Paula Danziger says, "The greatest times you can have with your teenagers still can involve play. Other than those two years—and you never know when they come—when your teenagers don't want anything to do with you, most of them love and admire parents who know how to have a good time. It's wonderful to continue to develop an adolescent's heightened sense of play. It's not bad to play as an adult, either. I speak to thousands of kids and get letters from them... and they want to have a good time with their parents."

That struck us as great advice if you can do it, if you can

---

*The New York Times* (September 8, 1986): B14.

keep using that kid part of you. If you're not comfortable being silly with your kids, invite adult friends over who are. We talked to many city parents who had friends that acted as surrogate uncles and aunts to their kids. These were often sin-

Taking time out from pressures and responsibilities. (PHOTO BY ROY MORSCH)

gle people, without families themselves, who related to kids and who became attached to their friends or their ex-lover's children. Said one mother, "I'm a bit of a formal type, but a lot of my friends are eccentrics who're great with my kids. In fact, I feel jealous sometimes."

Another mother added, "All kids need a parent or adult around who says no, but they also need one around who says 'Hey' and 'Yo.' There's nothing like the memory of that uncle who tapdanced in the Museum of Natural History or the grown-up who is addicted to pinball or video-game parlors.

Here is some specific advice for family times that city parents suggested to us:

## OUTSIDE

- Do any sporty thing together. It may seem obvious, but too many parents forget, as their kids grow into adolescence, that they would still love an afternoon bicycling or playing softball, volleyball or Frisbee with their folks; in cities, games may be harder to organize, but they're important. One father organized a weekly Saturday basketball game that fathers once played exclusively, but that adolescents became members of as they reached a certain age. "In our crowd, getting into the game was a rite of passage. And we almost never miss a Saturday. Maybe we don't talk enough, my son and I, but we'll always have this to look back on."

- If your adolescent likes art at all, go together. As Randy Williams of New York's Metropolitan Museum of Art said, "There is no one a teenager has more in common with than an artist who is searching to find out who he is and what life is about." A new exhibition, an opera, holography, modern dance, performance art, experimental music, avant-garde exhibits—all can be both educational and provide a chance for you and your teenager to talk and think together. And for kids who need their independence, attend separate exhibits or at least each go at your own pace—and then meet at the end for lunch.

- Establish a ritual of Sunday brunches or dinners together. Alternate responsibility for choosing the location—the middle of town or at a city park.
- If you're near water, check out any kind of fishing trip.

## HOME

"The more ceremonies you have and keep the better. We had family birthday celebrations, for us, for the kids, for the dog. We read poems. Rituals are wonderful," says Marie Winn.

Celebrate every holiday you can together. Said one mother, "I'm not religious, but I celebrated Hanukah for seven days. We not only lit a candle every day, but we read the same Hanukah stories each year or we read whatever was written in the papers that day about the holiday or we had friends over."

It helps to become involved in a community organization together. In the suburbs, a lot of social life revolves around the local church. For one city family, that didn't work, but the local Democratic club did. "There were always politicos around our house," this mother said. "They always talked to my son, and when he got bigger, he started debating them. They still came almost every Wednesday night, we played poker—and every once in a while, they'd let my son join them. He always tells us how he loved those evenings."

253

The simplest board games can be wonderful to play together as a family, even with adolescents: Trivial Pursuit or a mean game of Go or Monopoly. Taking out the old Sorry board and reverting to childhood can be the basis for a successful family evening.

Finally, consider story reading on a rainy night: a ghost story, a wonderful short story, a poem.

## BOREDOM, HANGING OUT, AND ADOLESCENTS ALONE IN THE CITY

Some teenagers, the ones with strong interests, have no trouble keeping busy. They hang out with friends, they pursue their passions. Many others, parents tell us, often don't know what to do with themselves on a Saturday or a Sunday. They aren't lucky enough to have developed a strong passion for something, they don't have one place to hang out, and they are tempted by either trouble or TV. And although occasional boredom isn't the worst thing in the world, it should be monitored.

Sometimes boredom, especially long-term boredom and lethargy, is a symptom of other things—depression, fears, inability to become engaged in life. A child who suffers such boredom may need psychological help. But sometimes, bored kids just need parental help. Said one mother, "Action is the ultimate question for my teenagers. The busier they are, the happier they seem. The happier they seem, the busier they become. Like anybody. But parents can help kids to act, can help them push that button that says, 'Now I'm going to do something.' "

How? Either you can spend time with them, doing any of the activities suggested in the previous section, or you can help them find activities to do by themselves or with friends. Here are a few suggestions:

- You can find or help establish a community center for teenagers to hang out in. See if a local public or private school can be open Saturdays or Sundays for kids to play ball in, for example. Can you build a constituency of parents to lobby for the rights of your kids? When the streets are safe, when parks are safe, teenagers will have no trouble finding places to hang out. That is the greatest loss for many modern city kids, and without a parents' lobby, without government recognizing that city kids, of all classes, are the core of a huge and vocal constituency, it will remain so.

- Find a community center with good leadership, whether it's a local Y or a church or a Jewish center. Find a parent whose son or daughter belongs, who knows your kid or will call her to invite her to a membership meeting of a particular team or club. Public school kids, especially, can't all be on school teams, don't become involved in school activities, and *need* a community group. To find it, parent networking is required. Ask everybody.

- "I gave up on finding a hangout," said one mother. "What I have done, though, is to teach my kids to be adventurous, to do things on their own. I put up a list in my kitchen every Friday, from the newspaper, magazines, recommendations of friends—the listings of what's doing in the city, from plays to happenings to great sales. We don't always do things, but I've tried to raise my kids with the notion that they can be bored and get out of it themselves by being a little resourceful. We're pretty energetic, too, so I have to

255

say that setting an example also helps. Maybe it's the most important thing of all."

## EXPENSE ACCOUNTS AND ACCOUNTS OF EXPENSES

City kids can cost more and more as they get older. Even when they go out alone, their entertainment is not just the high school steps or the local pizza joint, but adult city day and night spots. Said one parent, "It's not just that it costs much more, but I'm already sending him to a private school, to music lessons that are more expensive than they'd be someplace else, to sleepaway camps because staying in the city is the pits, so giving him a bigger allowance as he gets older just can be the straw that breaks the camel's back."

Not only can predictable expenses be a problem, such as for school lunches (when all his friends are buying, not bringing theirs) or for expensive transportation. City teenagers can have friends with widely varied parental incomes, and just as for adults, the temptations to keep up can confuse them. One single mother whose son went to a private high school felt terribly guilty that she couldn't offer her son more money to go to the clubs, the parties, the restaurants with $6.95 hamburgers that his best friend so easily managed. "Only in New York can two rich teenagers meet at a fancy spot for a $20 Saturday lunch. I couldn't afford that. But it wasn't easy. I felt if I told him I had money problems, I was 'hurrying him,' making him worry about my problems. But if I gave him more money, it created more financial problems for myself."

Says psychologist Sandra Mann, "Money doesn't have to be an ego problem if you look at it strictly as a management situation. You have so much money, you allocate it for essentials, you have so much left, and you allocate that based on your priorities and values."

Having money makes life easier anywhere, but parent after parent has told us that, along with space, it seems, unfortunately, particularly important in the city. Everything has a price: after-school activities, sports clubs, clothes, records, movies. Even transportation can account for $10 to $20 a week, especially if you're concerned about danger so that your children take cabs.

How do you arrive at a reasonable allowance? For a young teen, say experienced parents, simply add up the following: the cost of snacks, one movie, one pizza out a week, and one or two records or treats a month. Pay lunch and transportation costs separately as they come up because these expenses will make you think you're giving your children more spending money than they're really getting. The dollar amount can also become very high when those expenses are included, and young teens shouldn't have to become cost accountants.

You may easily wind up with an allowance of $15 to $25 a week. Is it reasonable? Are you being cheap? Among many of the professionals we spoke to, cheap is beautiful. Said Dr. Kelley, "Too many of the children I see are spoiled. They have allowances that are too big and parents who are too busy to keep track of what they do with the money. Give them chores, appropriate responsibilities, and money that will allow them to pay for a reasonable life-style. Controlling their income is a form of strictures, yes, but don't be afraid of it."

Or as a friend of ours and mother of three said, "Very few kids feel deprived of money if they're not deprived of love and attention. They may complain about it, feel poor, but if they feel loved, money is never a real issue."

## TEENAGERS AND EMPLOYMENT

As much as there is talk about "spoiled" and "fast-lane" teenagers, young adults spend more time working than their parents did. According to the *Harvard Education Letter* of September 1986, a third of *all* tenth graders now work, and another 25 percent of them are looking for work. Three out of five seniors in high school work. Inflation, longer hours, and higher minimum wages result in an astonishing fact: The average working high school senior puts in twenty hours a week, and takes home almost $300 a month. And although teenage income can relieve economic pressures on families and work does seem to broaden a youngster's life in many positive ways, there are, according to recent studies, factors to be aware of if your teenager is seeking work.

For one thing, family life can be affected. According to one study, working teenagers with less total time tend to take time away from family activities first. For another, grades may be affected. Experts suggest that the number of hours be limited. A high school sophomore, for example, should not work more than fifteen hours a week, and a senior not more than eighteen.

There have been no studies separating the work problems of city kids from others, but among city parents we spoke to, particularly urban issues did arise. It is hard for city kids to find work. Certain jobs are often class stereotyped: Middle-class city kids seem less likely to work at restaurant chains, such as Burger King, or city supermarkets, than suburban kids. Safety is a factor as well. Said one mother, "I don't want my daughter coming home at two in the morning from working at an ice cream parlor." Another said, "I don't like my son delivering groceries to apartments. It seems dangerous." These are city problems more than suburban ones. As a result, the jobs most favored by parents (and kids) tended to be more idiosyncratic: clerking in record stores, video shops, and health food stores; working at restaurants as bus boys or prep chefs or as waiters for local caterers; delivering flyers on the street for any cause or any store; helping out the superintendents of their building; or even walking dogs, offering juggling lessons, or providing entertainment at birthday parties.

The kids we spoke to had a variety of responses to their employment, depending on the job. The more entrepreneurial the work, the more they seemed to enjoy it. The larger, more impersonal the company, the more they complained about boredom, just as adults would.

If your child wants a job and is shy about pounding the pavement, parents suggest two approaches. The easiest, of course, is to encourage your kid to find a first job through his own friends or through yours. The second approach is to role-play with your youngster. Act out going into stores, with possible interview questions and responses.

Finally, consider one mother's thought: "I realized that working was a value we had, even though my kid didn't need the money. There was this myth that a young person should have a job, that earning money builds character. Well, maybe that's true. But then I thought, 'If we don't need the money and yet we feel Miles should work, there is one more option.' Through his school, there was a volunteering office. Kids could volunteer at the local city councilman's office, at a hospital, in a church that fed the homeless. Miles got a volunteer job through the Friends' School. He worked one afternoon a week reading to a blind woman. There was enough pressure on him to achieve—and, believe it or not—this was a job that actually gave him energy. He may not have earned anything in hard cash, but he felt like a million bucks."

## WHEN YOUR KID IS IN TROUBLE

Many parents reported that their kids went through a couple of very hard years. And although many kids and their city parents are more open about getting professional help, there are many teenagers who adamantly refuse to go.

How do you know when an adolescent needs help? Can you force him to get it? Dr. Arnold Cohen said, "You can't force a child to go to a therapist on a regular basis, but you can make him go the first time, especially if you all go. It helps if you emphasize that your teenager isn't in treatment, you're all in treatment, you all want help."

If a teenager refuses to see a counselor, *you* as parents can go. Modern theory has it that children often act out the problems of the whole family; therefore, couple or individual adult therapy can help. If that theory seem inapplicable in your case, then consider attending one of the parenting workshops that specialize in adolescence. Ellen Galinsky of the Bank Street College conducts seminars at corporations for working parents. "Even if the workshop is supposed to be about seven- to twelve-year-olds, it doesn't matter. The parents who come are always either new parents or parents of adolescents. They're the ones who feel most isolated and really need support groups." So consider them. They'll help you cope. (See the "Help for Parents" box earlier in this chapter for tips on holding workshops.)

## FINAL THOUGHTS

There are as many perspectives on raising city kids as there are parents. Here are a few final words:

*"It's harder when you're a single mother of a teenager. You have trouble letting go. You worry about their safety. But then there's usually some big rite of passage where you let them take a subway at eleven at night with three other kids, and they call you six times and that's it. You keep watch but you must let go. It's so wonderful; she's having such a wonderful time as a teenager here. But you still have to be available, you have to be supportive, and provide access."*

*"My house is a hangout for ten kids—they're tough and no one else wants them—they're unruly, uncooperative, ungainly, and unattractive, not to mention noisy. But they hang out here. You need patience. You need to relax. For example, teenagers are oily. Whatever they touch, they leave grease. I used to think it was from pizza. I think it comes from their bodies; it comes out of their fingers. Too many of them have been thrown out everywhere, are latchkey kids, like all over this country; but at least they have relatively safe outlets here, like my house, the park. Yes, there's marijuana here, and frankly I allow it. I smoke myself, and I think all this self-righteous talk about children being brought up like the old days is hypocritical and impossible."*

*"Now that Carrie's a teenager, it's hard to be together. We used to do everything together. Now if we're lucky, we have dinner. And then the phone rings. But those two minutes are quality time!"*

"*You know why happy city teenagers seem so wonderful and fearless and centered: The real world is their backyard. They're not on the periphery, intimidated to enter it later. Friends of mine have two daughters, eighteen and twenty. Their girls are just like the girls I remember at Yale who seemed so much luckier than me . . . I was a suburban kid. I have two little girls myself. I'd be proud to see them grow up as city kids.*"

# BIBLIOGRAPHY

## CHAPTER 6. CITY KIDS AT HOME

There are many good indoor activity books, and new ones coming out all the time. Here are some that mothers recommended or that we've browsed through or used ourselves:

Arnold, Arnold. *The World Book of Children's Games.* New York: World Books, 1972.

Cole, Ann, Carolyn Haas, et al., *I Saw A Purple Cow.* Boston: Little, Brown, 1972. This book describes crafts and activities for young children.

Educational Development Center: Pamphlets such as "Building with Cardboard," "Building with Tires," "Building with Tubes," Newton, Mass., Education Development Center.

Ferretti, Fred. *Baseball Card Flipping Guide.* New York: The New York Times Co., 1975.

Gustafson, Helen. *Dinner's Ready, Mom.* Berkeley: Celestial Arts, 1984. Krementz, Jill. *The Fun of Cooking.* New York: Alfred Knopf, 1985. Wilms, Barbara. *Crunchy Bananas.* Salt Lake City: Falcon Books, 1984. These are three good cookbooks for kids.

Hopper, Rita. *Rings, Swings and Climbing Things.* Chicago: Contemporary

Books, 1985. A terrific book on building your own indoor climbing devices. It's about gymnastics, so some of it won't apply to an apartment or appeal to a nonbuilder, but even if you're neither of these, the constructions are wonderful.

Kelly, Marguerite, and Elia Parsons. *The Mother's Almanac*. New York: Doubleday, 1975.

Quinn, Vernon. *Fifty Card Games for Children*. New York: Western Publishing, 1946.

Smith, Brian, and Shirley Sutton-Smith. *How to Play with your Children (And When Not To)*. New York: Hawthorn Books, Inc., and the Foley Agency, 1974.

Tembeck, Shoshana, and Andrew Fluegelman. *The New Games Book*. New York: Doubleday, 1976. Recommended by several parents.

Wiseman, Ann. *Making Things*. Boston: Little, Brown, 1973; and *More Making Things*. Boston: Little, Brown, 1975. Very popular crafts books.

## CHAPTER 10. NATURAL RESOURCES

### Magazines

*National Geographic World* (the magazine's version for children). Contact the National Geographic Society, Seventeenth and M streets NW, Washington, DC 20036

*Owl* magazine (for children ages seven to twelve). Contact Young Naturalist Foundation, 59 Front Street E, Toronto, Ontario, Canada 1B3 COR

*Ranger Rick* (for kids ages six to twelve); or *Your Big Backyard* (for kids ages three to five). Contact the National Wildlife Federation, 1412 16th Street NW, Washington, DC 20036.

### Nature Books For Kids And Parents

The American Camping Association issues a catalogue of nature books every year. You can order through its toll-free number, (800) 428-CAMP, or write to the American Camping Association Bookstore, Bradford Woods, 5000 State Road 67 North, Martinsville, Indiana 46151-7902.

Every December, *Scientific American* reviews science books for kids and these include many nature books. They are very accessible and helpful summaries of what's new and good each year and tend to really be oriented to what kids will actually like and learn from.

Some good choices include:

*Books for Young Explorers*. Washington, DC: National Geographic Society.

This series offers beautifully photographed books on various nature topics for children.

Cassells, Sylvia. *Games and Activities.* New York: Harper and Row, 1956. A good source of nature games for kids.

Cornell, Joseph. *Sharing Nature with Children.* Nevada City, CA: Ananda Publications, 1979.

Gallob, Edward. *City Rocks, City Blocks, and the Moon.* New York: Charles Scribners Sons, 1973. Great for mineral collectors or for looking at city structures and understanding what they're made of.

*Golden Nature Books,* and *Golden Field Guides.* New York: Western Publishing. These guides are small, easy to carry, and have waterproof covers. The author of each guide is an expert on the topic.

The Natural Science for Youth Foundation (11 Wildwood Valley, NE; Atlanta, Georgia 30338) publishes biographies of great naturalists, including *In the Steps of Carl Ethan Akley, the Great Museum Collector; In the Steps of the Great American Entomologist, Frank Eugene Lutz; In the Steps of the Zoologist William Temple Hornaday;* and others. They also copublish, with *Reader's Digest, Favorite Nature Stories.*

Rey, H. A. *The Stars: A New Way to See Them.* Boston: Houghton Mifflin, 1970. Christopher Cerf, one of the authors of *Kids Day In, Day Out* says that this book "changed my life." Rey is the author of the Curious George books, and the book has cartoons, amusing comments, and pictures of the constellations that really look like something instead of some abstract fill-in-the-dots. For kids ages ten and over.

Russell, Franklin. *Watchers at the Pond.* New York: Alfred Knopf, 1961. This is a classic.

Shuttlesworth, Dorothy. *Exploring Nature With Your Child.* New York: Abrams, 1977.

Simon, Seymour. *Pets in a Jar* and *Look to the Night Sky.* New York: Puffin Books, 1979. Talbott Spence of Wave Hill Public Gardens highly recommends Simon's city nature books. Kids enjoy them, and they are very helpful in Wave Hill's programs.

Stein, Sara B. *Great Pets.* New York: Workman Publishing, 1976.

*Zoobooks.* Each publication in this series is devoted to a different animal. Contact Wildlife Education, Ltd., 930 W. Washington Street, San Diego, California 92103.

## CHAPTER 12. CITY MINDS, CITY VALUES

Here is some literature that might help you, as a parent, deal with the complex issues of raising a child in the city.

Clark, Kenneth B. *Prejudice and Your Child*. Boston: Beacon Press, 1963.

Coles, Robert. *The Moral Life of Children*. Boston: The Atlantic Monthly Press, 1986.

Elkind, David. *All Grown Up and No Place to Go*. Reading, Mass: Addison-Wesley, 1984.

———*The Hurried Child*. Reading, Mass. Addison-Wesley, 1982.

Gordon, S., and J. Gordon. *Raising a Child Conservatively in a Sexually Permissive World*. New York: Simon & Schuster, 1983.

Porter, Judith D.R. *Black Child, White Child; The Development of Racial Attitudes*. Boston: Harvard University Press, 1971.

Postman, Neil. *The Disappearance of Childhood*. New York: Delacorte, 1982.

Schulman, M., and E. Mekler. *Bringing Up a Moral Child: A New Approach for Teaching Your Child to Be Kind, Just, and Responsible*. Reading, Mass: Addison-Wesley, 1985.

Winn, Marie. *Children Without Childhood*. New York: Penguin, 1984.

# ABOUT THE AUTHORS

**SUSAN HAVEN** has written about children for *The New York Times, Redbook, New York, Ms.,* and *Woman's Day.* She has written two children's books and an ABC Afterschool Special, and she created material for Lily Tomlin's "Edith Ann." She edited Margaret Mead's *Culture and Commitment,* as well as the collected works of British child psychologist Margaret Lowenthal. She was raised in Brooklyn, New York, and lives in Manhattan with her husband and fifteen-year-old son.

**VALERIE MONROE** has been an editor at *Ms., Viva,* and *Redbook* magazines. She has written for *Glamour, Working Woman,* and *Ms.,* and for two years she wrote a monthly column for *Redbook.* She lives in New York City with her husband and three-year-old son.